DESIGN AND CONSTRUCTION IN ROMANESQUE ARCHITECTURE

In this study, C. Edson Armi offers a fresh interpretation of Romanesque architecture. Armi focuses on buildings in southern France, northern Italy, Catalonia, and Switzerland, the regions where Romanesque architecture first appeared around A.D. 1000. He integrates the study of medieval structure with an understanding of construction, decoration, and articulation in an effort to determine the origins and originality of medieval architecture and the formation of the High Romanesque style, especially in Burgundy, at sites such as Cluny III. Relying on a close analysis of the fabric of key buildings, Armi's in-depth study reveals new knowledge about design decisions in the early Middle Ages. It also demonstrates that the mature Romanesque of the twelfth century continues many of the applications created and perfected over the previous one hundred years.

C. Edson Armi is a professor at the Department of History of Art and Architecture at the University of California, Santa Barbara. A scholar of medieval art and architecture, he is the author of the prizewinning *Masons and Sculptors in Romanesque Burgundy* and *The "Headmaster" of Chartres and the Origins of "Gothic" Sculpture.*

DESIGN AND CONSTRUCTION IN ROMANESQUE ARCHITECTURE

First Romanesque Architecture and the Pointed Arch in Burgundy and Northern Italy

C. EDSON ARMI

University of California, Santa Barbara

CAMBRIDGE
UNIVERSITY PRESS

PUBLISHED BY THE PRESS SYNDICATE OF THE UNIVERSITY OF CAMBRIDGE
The Pitt Building, Trumpington Street, Cambridge, United Kingdom

CAMBRIDGE UNIVERSITY PRESS
The Edinburgh Building, Cambridge CB2 RU, UK
40 West 20th Street, New York, NY 10011–4211, USA
477 Williamstown Road, Port Melbourne, VIC 3166, Australia
Ruiz de Alarcón 13, 28014 Madrid, Spain
Dock House, The Waterfront, Cape Town 8001, South Africa

http://www.cambridge.org

First published 2004

Printed in the United Kingdom at the University Press, Cambridge

Typeface Meridien 10.5/14.5 pt.   *System* Quark XPress™   [MG]

A catalog record for this book is available from the British Library

Library of Congress Cataloging-in-Publication Data available
Armi, C. Edson.
Design and construction in Romanesque architecture / C. Edson Armi.
p.   cm.
Includes bibliographical references and index.
ISBN 0-521-83033-8 (hb)
Architecture, Romanesque.   I. Title.
NA390.A76 2004
723´.4 – dc21
2003048553

ISBN 0 521 83033 8 hardback

Contents

6

Systems of Arch Support *113*

7

The Pointed Arch and the Context of High Romanesque
Architecture in Burgundy *139*

Conclusion *177*

Illustrations

FIGURES

DRAWINGS

Acknowledgments

I would like to confess that at eighteen I suddenly fell in love with Romanesque architecture, and the passion has stayed with me forever. Unfortunately, while the last part of this statement may be true, the first part, however romantic, is fundamentally distorted. The undergraduate art-history teachers at Columbia University initiated and nourished my interest in Romanesque architecture, and thoroughly shaped my approach to it. I must begin a book on this subject by thanking them.

As a sophomore I took a class on early medieval art with someone who was more than what usually is called an inspiring teacher. Although a university professor, Meyer Schapiro took the time to shepherd small groups of undergraduates to see medieval manuscripts at the Morgan Library. However much these books touched me, the interaction of this man with art impressed me even more. At this point in my studies I dared not approach him personally. Nevertheless, his love of the object, his approach to writing about art, and the insights he brought to creation opened not only a field of research but also – may I say it without sounding trite – a way of being and a life commitment. From him, at a very young age, I realized what art history could be.

To whet our appetite for high medieval art, on the last day of class Schapiro showed one slide of the central tympanum at Vézelay. He used it to criticize Henri Focillon's theory that the pressure exerted by architecture determined the shape of Romanesque sculpture. This black-and-white image did not knock me off my feet, but I believe that a small epiphany did occur, and I trace an interest in the specific problems of Burgundian Romanesque architecture and sculpture to this moment in a dark classroom. I also believe that, right from the start, his patient and layered method of looking and his tendency to integrate the discussion of sculpture and architecture (as a young man he had seriously considered being an architect) influenced my thinking about Romanesque art. Schapiro showed remarkable sensitivity to the creative role of masons and sculptors within the group activity of church building. This approach that balances the individual expression of possibly illiterate artisans against the group dynamics of a structured organization inspired me to study the creative process in medieval art and industrial design.

During my sophomore year, I was advised that learning German and French was necessary to become an art historian. My German-born parents had wanted me to have a positive appreciation of German culture, and so for three summers between my fifth and eleventh birthdays, I had lived in Germany, learned German, and presumably, at some now forgotten locations, seen Romanesque churches. After my experience with Vézelay, however, the incentive to learn another language became secondary to the need to see beautiful Romanesque buildings. At the end of the school year, I took the money set aside for acquiring French, bought a motorbike and a sleeping bag, and enrolled at the University of Grenoble. I then quickly motored off to spend the summer visiting Romanesque churches all over France. I studied and drew them and often slept in the bushes next to them, but I never properly learned French grammar.

On my return to college, I convinced Philip MacAleer, who was scheduled to teach Gothic architecture, that it would make sense to lay the foundation with a course on Romanesque architecture. As one of the few American experts in Romanesque architecture, he did not have to be persuaded to change the content of this class. Although young, he was a formidable teacher, and the way he presented Romanesque architecture had a formative impact. Lecturing without notes, he made the content precise and spare, and structured lessons as carefully as Bach arranged a fugue. He underscored the seriousness and worthiness of this arcane discipline by subjecting each scholar to devastating criticism, presenting each building complexly and in detail, and delicately placing each art-historical problem in its historical context.

At Columbia College, there were not only two Romanesque specialists to train me in my chosen field but also teachers whose approach to the art of other periods I found sympathetic. I was raised in a family of physicists, and I enjoyed seeing the physical evidence that supported ideas. Under the leadership of Rudolf Wittkower, Columbia had become a center for positivist research. He did not teach undergraduate courses, but the college allowed me to enroll in his graduate classes (as well as those of George Collins, another outstanding architectural historian). I was strongly influenced by Wittkower's interests in the creativity of the individual, the relationship between one person's work in different media, and the changing character within an architect's oeuvre. The specificity, depth, order, and pace Wittkower brought to the examination of Renaissance and baroque buildings struck me. To this day, I cannot think or write about architecture without being reminded of the standards he set for himself.

His standard of thoroughness literally took my breath away. He lectured for two hours in a room that faced Amsterdam Avenue, and although these classes were standing room only, he allowed no breaks or open windows, for fear that the traffic noise might interrupt the flow of the material. By the end of class, it was not unusual for students to faint from heat exhaustion and the loss of air. I learned to tape his lectures, a technique that in graduate school allowed me to follow two other exacting, no-holds-barred architectural historians, Robert Branner and Richard Krautheimer.

As chairman, Wittkower encouraged connoisseurship, and Howard Davis at Columbia College and Evelyn Harrison and Julius Held at Barnard College (the women's college of Columbia University) pursued this approach with astonishing levels of sophistication. Raised in a slow-paced California beach town, as a college student I often walked around Manhattan barefoot and skateboarded on the streets leading to Riverside Drive. I hardly expected competition just to get a good look at a slide. On the first day of class with Harrison and Held, I showed up at a time that I assumed was early, only to discover outside the door row after row of jostling mink coats containing Barnard commuters vying for front-row seats to get the best view of the art. Under these two professors (and the patient guidance of Bill Voekle, Held's teaching assistant), I began to understand that the physical examination of art is not a superficial activity. At the deepest level it could be a strenuous and time-consuming search that requires sensitivity, training, and experience to be carried out successfully. To this day, when I plant myself in a building or repeatedly return to the same visual problem, I think of these and other undergraduate teachers, and I am profoundly grateful to them.

Returning to the present, I thank Beatrice Rehl, Michael Gnat, and the anonymous readers of Cambridge University Press for many important suggestions for improving the text. The work of free-lance proofreaders Susana Galilea, Nina McCune, and Winifred Davis was also most helpful. I also thank Larry Ayres, Jim Morganstern, and Elizabeth B. Smith for their comradery and insights into Romanesque architecture, Marie-Claude Reboux for her friendship and support, and above all, my wife, Mary, and daughters, Jemma and Rovenna, for their love and patience. Mary encouraged, questioned, and criticized my ideas, and edited parts of the manuscript in front of the buildings. At the University of California, medieval graduate students Cindy Canejo, Michelle Duran-McLure, Holly Henderson, Vibeke Olson, and Sarah Thompson were of immeasurable help in resolving problems in this book.

I deeply appreciate the financial support provided for this project from a John Simon Guggenheim Memorial Foundation Fellowship, a Paul Mellon Senior Visiting Fellowship at the Center for Advanced Study in the Visual Arts (National Gallery), and grants from the Graham Foundation for Advanced Studies in the Fine Arts and the Research Council of the University of California.

Introduction

I

This book is about a specific architectural feature, the pointed arch. The subject can be elusive, however, because early Romanesque vaults often are irregular and their shapes hard to define. When I use the term *pointed web*, I usually describe something loosely characterized as the extension at the peak of a web where it rises over an arcade, wall arch, or transverse arch on the side of a vault. This extension may be broken, but often it resembles the tip of a catenary cord, as opposed to the intersection of equal curves or the regular outline of an ellipse.[1] More broadly speaking, however, this book is about the creative context of vault construction in Romanesque architecture in southern Europe.

In the first part of the twentieth century, Romanesque architecture was a topic of interest in America. Two successive Harvard professors, Arthur Kingsley Porter and his student Kenneth Conant, pioneered the field with groundbreaking studies on Lombard and Cluniac architecture; at Columbia, Meyer Schapiro reframed the major questions of Romanesque monumental art; and at the Metropolitan Museum, James Rorimer with the help of John D. Rockefeller Jr. created one of the outstanding collections of Romanesque architectural sculpture.

In the second part of the century, Americans turned a cold shoulder to this subject. The major museums in New York, Philadelphia, Boston, and Cambridge that had previously competed for the best Romanesque pieces almost stopped acquiring them. After Conant wrote his survey in 1959, no major book was written in English on Romanesque architecture.[2] The lack of interest to a certain extent existed worldwide. After Josep Puig i Cadafalch in 1935 completed *La Géographie et les origines du premier art roman,* no one in any language studied together the hundreds of early eleventh-century churches in the southern littoral of Europe;[3] and for three-quarters of a century, virtually nothing was written about the building and structure of Romanesque vaults.[4]

I would like to contribute to these three little-studied areas of research: early medieval vault construction and structure, international First Romanesque architecture, and the transition to later medieval forms of building. Specifically, I use the pointed arch and the principles of arch and vault construction to study First Romanesque architecture and its impact on High Romanesque architecture. Within a building, I ask: Why did masons use the point, where did they use it, and how did they use it? The answers to these questions will tell us something about the creativity of the artists, the tradition from which they worked, and the relation of structure to other aspects of building – like construction and aesthetics.

Throughout southern Europe at the beginning of the eleventh century, the pointed arch was used as an important part of groin-vault construction in architecture built with bricks and stones the shape of brick. This discovery leads me to a number of conclusions about First and High Romanesque architecture. Masons who built the earliest brick-based churches did not focus only on thick walls with superficial, banded decoration. They also explored the point of support at the base of groin vaults, especially in combination with sophisticated pointed webs and relieving arches. In Burgundy at the beginning of the eleventh century, masons expanded this system by combining the point support of groin vaults with the continuous support of barrel vaults used extensively inside and between walls. They created complicated and innovative designs, including a type of elevation that allows an unusual combination of light, space, and proportions. In the largest sense, then, I use the pointed arch to investigate not only the creative process but also the shared heritage and diversity of approaches within the tradition of brick-based construction.

II

It frequently has been suggested that Romanesque architecture is a massive style of building with small openings and round-headed arches.[5] According to this theory, only at the turn of the twelfth century did masons find the means to avoid the limitations imposed by static walls and continuous lateral pressure inherent in the barrel vault. They then built high, light, and airy structures that depend on the point support of groin webs and pointed arches.

This rags-to-riches story of medieval architecture often culminates in the Paris basin with masons who were predisposed to thin walls. They invented the Gothic style by combining the pointed arch from Burgundy with the rib vault from Normandy. Whether true or not, this theory about the sources of Gothic architecture does not explain why and where Burgundian masons in the eleventh century first used the pointed arch and vault.

If, as I claim, Burgundian masons used the point well before the twelfth century, did they use it in isolation or as part of a long-standing building tradition? Moreover, to what degree did they use international sources, regional tradition, and their own creativity to exploit the pointed arch in buildings as important as Cluny III? The answers to these questions are the focus of this book.

III

Creative "firsts" often are used to explain important steps in the history of art. In the history of medieval architecture, the pointed arch along with the statue column and flying buttress have received this kind of landmark status. Writers often consider these innovations as restrictive typological devices; discuss them separately from the broad context of labor, construction, and articulation; and locate the first appearance of these devices in large and prestigious French buildings. The first flying buttress, for example, is said to debut in the cathedral of Notre Dame, Paris, and the statue column in the royal abbey at Saint-Denis.[6]

As the largest church in Christendom, Cluny III has garnered its share of firsts. The style of the ambulatory capitals and the soaring proportions of the interior often are described as breakaway achievements. Similarly, it is claimed the pointed arch appeared in northern Europe for the first time after 1088 in the arcades, transverse arches, and central vault at the mother church (Fig. 1).[7] At dispute is the exact journey the pointed arch took before it reached southern Europe from areas of Arab domination. Generally it is believed that the device first appeared after 1050 at Italian sites like Amalfi and Monte Cassino.[8]

To explain the first appearance of the pointed arch in northern Europe, scholars often cite as a cause the search for efficient support at the end of the eleventh and beginning of the twelfth centuries.[9] As masons sought to make the barrel vault stronger and lighter, they introduced devices like the pointed arch to channel weight efficiently. This notion, that builders continuously solved problems, and as a result introduced structural improvements, complements the view of the history of medieval architecture as a series of typological firsts that occurred at important and increasingly more sophisticated churches.

A method that explains the evolution of medieval structure in terms of the logical introduction of new devices is convenient and handy because very few historical texts explain changes in medieval architecture. There is a downside to this approach, however, since if used by itself, it may be taken to imply that problems of structural change can be isolated and understood apart from other considerations.

Because the creative process of early Romanesque architecture is essentially undocumented, I have developed a methodology to begin to answer causal questions by examining the remaining physical evidence.[10] I use this method to analyze the pointed arch in the broad context of building. A thorough examination of a building requires more than making an archaeological inventory or establishing typological groupings, as is often the custom in France. What is needed is an approach that couples a precise and complex analysis of material, shape, size, and finish with an understanding of construction, structure, and the relationship of parts. To fill the void left by a lack of written evidence, I concentrate on masonry – its consistencies and inconsistencies – to appreciate the hand of the mason on the stone. I do this in an attempt to re-create the design and building process and to document

1. Cluny III, interior, nave, J.-B. Lallemand, 1773.

the decisions that masons made in the context of a specific tradition of labor. In my own work I make an effort to put a face on creation – that is, to associate individuals, workshops, and building traditions with a comprehensive physical understanding of works of art. I have never understood the common practice of isolating issues of form, authorship, and meaning from a collective consideration of material, construction, and structure, or the widespread Anglo-American approach of discussing Romanesque stone sculpture apart from architectural issues.

Based on an approach that considers structure together with material, construction, articulation, and decoration, I draw new conclusions about when, where, and under what circumstances masons introduced changes in medieval vaulting. The use of the point appeared widely in the context of the earliest Romanesque architecture in the Mediterranean basin – and not, as previously thought, at the turn of the twelfth century in the context of Burgundian High Romanesque architecture. In these early eleventh-century buildings, masons used the pointed arch predominantly in groin vaults, not in barrel vaults as is so often claimed. With the help of pointed webs, they could make groin vaults light and thin, and incorporate the vault into a sophisticated system of structure, construction, and aesthetics.

In both northern Italy and Burgundy, masons in the eleventh century used a brick technique to build pointed vaults. In each region, however, very different lessons were taken from these experiments. In the side aisles of northern Italian churches, masons often pointed groin webs but kept the arches – the arcades, transverse arches, and *formerets* – semicircular. In the center of the nave, these round-headed arches are often coupled with a wooden ceiling or a round-headed rib vault. In Burgundy, in contrast, masons often vaulted the nave and expanded the use of pointed arches throughout the building. Not only are groin webs pointed, but likewise frequently the arcades, *formerets*, transverse arches, and even the barrel vaults in the center of the nave.

IV

The discovery that masons had used the pointed arch with an active system of arch support throughout the littoral of Europe from the beginning of the eleventh century prompts a question: How does one frame the broader issue of change in medieval architecture?

Southern First Romanesque architecture has frequently been regarded as a primitive and folkloric stop on the road to high medieval architecture. Since the writings of Porter and Puig i Cadafalch, this early eleventh-century architecture has continued to be labeled as structurally unadventuresome and aesthetically limited.[11] Puig i Cadafalch maintained that First Romanesque builders followed a "blind and unconscious routine . . , because of the lack of any rational mechanical system of calculating stability and resistance . . . and because of the self-complacency of those who believed themselves subject to an unchanging discipline." As a result, forms that before the First Romanesque period were "originally architectonic gradually tended to become decorative. . . . [T]hey had no longer the constructive logic of their form, and became bulk and mass, playthings of the decorator, pure line, undefined space, baroque." This structural and aesthetic crisis was resolved only when "the more far-seeing and more intelligent architects of the twelfth century" superseded with "great compositions" the "popular, modest, poverty-stricken elements of the first Romanesque style."[12]

Pierre Truchis, Charles Oursel, and Jean Virey, the leading specialists of early Romanesque architecture in Burgundy, described the earliest brick-based buildings there as massive and inactive, and Oursel and Virey further suggested that folkloric artisans overbuilt these churches because they feared the vaults might collapse.[13] According to this theory, masons anxious about vaulting created rigid and bulky walls, lined with superficial ornament, instead of lighter envelopes that resisted vault pressure through point support and vaults inside the wall. Dreading the effect of vault weight, early Burgundian masons engaged, in Oursel's words, in a "vicious circle" that produced piled-up material rather than a complicated interrelation of vault, wall, space, and light: "Our architects of the eleventh century essentially demanded stability and containment of material." Being disposed to support the weight of vaults with mass, the earliest Burgundian masons preferred to make "walls . . . enormous, pillars bulky, arches thick and crude, doors small, . . . openings reduced. . . . The whole is heavy and weighty, and if one wishes to make it bigger, one risks also to make it heavier and weightier, to augment the pressures, and thus also the mass which must contain them. It is a vicious circle."[14]

To overcome this self-defeating circle in which fearful builders produced architecture "imprisoned in mass," Burgundian masons, Oursel and Virey agreed, needed help from the outside, specifically from internationally trained architects who designed Cluny III: "It is, in one word, a primitive or primary art, that hardly knew by its own means how to exit from itself. But, at the end of the eleventh century, owing to Cluny, Burgundian architecture succeeded in escaping from itself."[15]

This negative picture of the structure of brick-based buildings has become common in scholarship devoted to the broad range of early eleventh-century architecture.[16] New information about systems of support may help to change the image of these churches from static, massive, and superficially ornamented buildings – gawky and unprogressive foils to the revolutionary genius at Cluny III – to creative, complicated, and interactive structures.

In particular, the new evidence showing an early date and context of the pointed arch makes it difficult to teach students that medieval architecture evolved from thick walls and round-headed vaults to light, pointed skeletal construction. The notion of twelfth-century architecture as a breakthrough to a delicate, spacious, point-support system has tended to overshadow the sophisticated system of pointed groin vaults that preceded it by one hundred years in Lombardy, Catalonia, and Burgundy. Moreover, the discovery that this early tradition of southern European vault construction continued with renewed life throughout the eleventh century in Burgundy supports the argument for the existence of a progressive and structurally sophisticated High Romanesque architecture in this region. In the vicinity of Cluny, by the end of the eleventh century masons had created their own delicate, lighted, and spacious form of building.

CHAPTER

1

History, Geography, and Construction

The Franco-Provençal [transalpine] domain . . . is not
a land, it is not a nation; it is a route, it is a town.
— Pierre Gardette

 At the beginning of the twentieth century, the art historians Raffaele Cattaneo, Ferdinand Daltein, Arthur Kingsley Porter, Josep Puig i Cadafalch, and Giovanni Rivoira argued that Lombard masons, aided by transplanted Italian abbots like William of Volpiano, influenced the appearance of northern French High Romanesque architecture.[1] The thesis of a Lombard–northern French axis has been criticized, modified, and amplified; but no one has succeeded in disproving the idea that Italian masons, by themselves or through intermediaries, transmitted the techniques of Lombard structure, construction, and ornamentation to early eleventh-century architecture in Burgundy.[2]

Specific cultural and geographic reasons explain how Lombard masons and their ideas could easily penetrate the Alps and descend through the region of the Jura to the edge of the Mâconnais, in southern Burgundy (Fig. 2). For centuries following the collapse of the Roman Empire, this transalpine area east of the Saône River and west of the Aosta pass was politically united. Burgundian settlers, who originally came from Scandinavia and then moved westward through Poland and southern Germany, controlled, by the middle of the fifth century, the land between Lake Geneva, the Jura, the northern Dauphiné, and the Franche-Comté.[3]

During the fifth century, the Merovingian Franks annexed this area, but during the next three centuries they preserved Burgundy as a separate and intact kingdom.[4] Even after the empire had absorbed the transalpine area following Charlemagne's death, political and cultural links continued in the region. In the tenth century, the counts of Mâcon on the local feudal level ruled the territory from the Saône River to the Jura Mountains, and maintained tight connections within this domain.[5] The people of the Kingdom of Burgundy also preserved their independence through a separate language.[6] From the tenth century, in a region extending from the Alps beyond the Saône River, inhabitants universally spoke a transalpine dialect that was different from the *oïl* in northern France and the *oc* in southern France.[7] Even as recently as three generations ago, over three million people continued to use this vernacular.[8]

The transalpine geography between Italy and France allows for open exchange among people. The territory has no natural frontiers, and roads and river highways unite it.[9] Geological formations create a climate conducive to travel. In particular, high peaks partially shield the Valley of Aosta from exterior influences, and they provide a dry strip wider than in any other interior region of the Alps.[10] This unique topography acts as both a protective cell and an intersection.

This double function of the valley is reinforced by the major routes running through it.[11] The western borders overlap the Rhône–Saône basin, a vast and natural transportation route that directly connects Geneva and the Alpine passes with Lyons and the Mediterranean Sea. In the eleventh century, major roads surviving from the Roman period linked the Valley of Aosta with the Jura and ensured communication between both sides of the mountains in the region.[12] The Franco-Provençal linguistic expert Pierre Gardette explained that the two most important Roman roads from Lyons (the capital of Gaul) to Rome paralleled the arms of a triangle that inscribed this Franco-Provençal-speaking region (see Fig. 2): "The route created a unity, dispersing legends, songs, no doubt words, and perhaps a language in the process of formation. In any case it created a social unity which must have persisted when Rome no longer was Rome."[13] As speakers of the Franco-Provençal patois easily moved along these highways from the Rhône basin to the Po basin, they came to dominate the clergy and upper classes on both sides of Mont Blanc.[14]

In addition to the bonds of language, culture, and geography that united both sides of the Alps, changes in social structure and the econ-

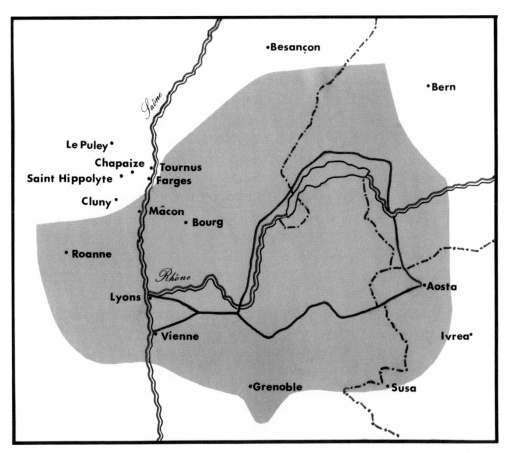

2. Map of the Franco-Provençal dialect in the eleventh century, after Pierre Gardette, *Études de géographie linguistique,* Strasbourg, 1983, 612. *Gray area:* approximate limit of the Franco-Provençal dialect; *unbroken line:* major Roman roads surviving in the eleventh century; *broken line:* current borders of France, Italy, and Switzerland.

omy encouraged masons to travel and work across the southern littoral of Europe at the beginning of the eleventh century. In the past twenty-five years, the leading historians of the Mâconnais, Provence, and Catalonia have come to agree that in these regions a new order was beginning to emerge at this time.[15] Scholars like Guy Bois, Pierre Bonnassie, Georges Duby, Robert Fossier, and Jean-Pierre Poly base their conclusions on detailed analysis of population, trade, habitation, and religious and social institutions.

Around the year 1000, the population along the southern littoral of Europe exploded as villages increased in size and number. People needed new churches.[16] The expansion began about 930 in the Po Valley and Catalonia, slightly later in Provence, and after 1000 in the Saône Valley.[17] In the Mâconnais, by the end of the tenth century all classes engaged in what Georges Duby described as "demographic vigor."[18] In Catalonia, the high density and heterogeneous influx of immigrants fleeing Muslim control contributed to the dynamic economy and cultural vitality of the region.[19]

It is a particular irony that this "triumph of localism," as Robert Lopez labeled it, encouraged internationalism in building.[20] Across southern Europe, power, both judicial and military, increasingly devolved to local sovereigns instead of to the central authority of the Carolingian court.[21] The spiritual hopes of these local lords, expressed through donations to the church, often went hand in hand with the financial needs of nearby monks.[22] In turn monasticism, through religious reform and the control it exercised over property, caused an enormous resurgence in church building.[23] In Catalonia, between 950 and 1050 twenty new monasteries were built; in the Mâconnais, by the eleventh century the Cluniac Order sizably expanded its building program.[24] To give an idea of the resources of the order in this region, after the year 1000, about 40 percent of the cultivated land belonged to the church, principally represented by Cluny.[25] Jerrilynn Dodds has connected the rise of the local power of feudal lords and the expanded influence of monasteries with the international impact of brick-based architecture at the turn of the eleventh century. She gives new insights into the roles masons and monks played in propagating this style: "The dissolution of the sovereignty of a number of kings distributed power and wealth to new feudal lords who passed both along to the great monasteries, which became the repository of the old royal prerogatives of pomp and patronage." These newly rich and powerful lords and monks often left aesthetic decisions in the hands of masons. By deferring to skilled specialists, these new patrons "stimulated a craftsman's style, which by virtue of the peripatetic nature of the masons' trade and the lively new market for their craft, spread throughout Italy, Switzerland, and southern France."[26] The international orientation of important abbots like Odillo and Oliba, who sponsored monastic construction in southern Europe at the beginning of the eleventh century, also opened the way for a style of building that did not originate locally in Catalonia or Burgundy.[27]

By the year 1000, the threat of Saracen attacks along the coastland disappeared, allowing unhindered passage by masons across Italy, the Alps, and Provence. Previously, these marauders had periodically harassed, abducted, and plundered the population along the Mediterranean coastland.[28] In 985 they sacked Barcelona; by the tenth century they had established a base at Garde-Freinet, near Nice;[29] and between 921 and 942, they made ten raids in the passes of the Alps.[30] In 940 Saracens had occupied Saint-Maurice-d'Agaume on the Grand-Saint-Bernard route, and in 972 they even captured for ransom the Cluniac Abbot Mayeul on his way home from Rome.[31] By the turn of the century, however, not only had the Saracens been cleared from the southern littoral, but the power of the Carolingian authorities had also been shown to be weak in the face of the threat. The result was that control increasingly fell to local feudal lords, like Guinebaud de Brancion and Ramon Borrell in Catalonia, who began to maintain a high degree of military, social, and financial control in their districts.[32] The reduced threat also meant that travel along the passes from Lombardy became much more fluid, so those monasteries along these routes prospered and expanded.[33]

At this time the exchange of work for pay, instead of for goods, became common as gold and currency in general increasingly transformed the labor market.[34] In the Mâconnais, by the eleventh century money had penetrated into the furthest reaches of the countryside and supported the growth of rural trade.[35] In Catalonia, the growth of trade was stimulated after 980 by the massive introduction of Muslim gold currency.[36] Very little gold had been mined in Europe, so that the influx of gold from outside combined with the local minting of precious metals became the "motor" that drove the local feudal society.[37] Lords could now use money to support a military force, and the church could hire builders from anywhere, who were able to spend their earnings elsewhere.[38] The daily use of currency, and the fluidity that it created in the market, fostered social mobility.

The conjunction of increased population, thriving local economies, vigorous monastic reform, and the elimination of the Saracen threat meant that builders could travel unimpeded, receive pay in negotiable currency, and find work in the local economies that prospered throughout southern Europe. It comes as no surprise that the reputation of Lombard builders soon impressed church patrons on the other side of the Alps. A measure of the strength of this impact is that brick-based construction, entrenched for centuries in northern Italy, came to dominate southern European stone architecture.[39] The influence of Lombard brick construction, as a system of building, to a large extent explains the birth of Romanesque architecture in southern Europe, not only in terms of the general aesthetic (the shape and dimensions of the stone, and the articulation of masonry) but also in terms of the structural devices used to stabilize and reinforce stone buildings.

In much of northern Italy, as Porter explained, masons had few options other than to build with brick, because quarried stone usually was unavailable.[40] Building with brick had had a long tradition in this region. In the Early Christian period, masons had made large Milanese churches, like San Lorenzo and San Simpliciano, entirely of brick, and in the early eleventh century, particularly in major cities, masons followed this tradition.[41] Among the best known of these early eleventh-century brick buildings are San Vincenzo in Milan, the cathedral of Ivrea, the chevet of Sant'Ambrogio in Milan, and the tower of the cathedral of Novara (Fig. 3).

In churches like these in Lombardy and the Piedmont, masons developed a special form of construction, structure, and wall design that reflects the character of brick. In the tower at Novara, regular horizontal courses repeat the shape and size of bricks and cause the mass of the building to appear uninterrupted, despite vertical openings and interruptions.[42] Rectangular bricks line round-headed door and window openings, and uniform brick courses continue right through corners, bands, and door and window jambs. The squared brick edge also joins the parts of the building on the exterior and interior. On the exterior, there are no horizontal interruptions caused by projecting imposts and stringcourse moldings; instead, at each level, the arcades in the corbel table horizontally connect each other and, without the interruption of moldings, vertically join the square-edged reveals of Lombard bands. Similarly on the interior, the squared-off *dosserets* and arcade orders connect, without horizontal projecting moldings, to analogous square-

3. Novara, cathedral, exterior, northern transept tower, brickwork.

edged reveals in the compound piers at the base of the nave. New capitals were made for the crypts at Oleggio and Agliate (Figs. 4, 5), but often, as in the nave at Agliate, decoration was reused. In either case, southern masons preferred to connect each side of the arcade, impost, and capital as a smooth surface, without interrupting it with a projecting, wraparound molding.

In contrast, in northern France at the turn of the eleventh century, masons did not use regular and continuous beds of bricklike stones.

4. Oleggio, San Michele, interior, crypt, central and southern aisles; (*a*) corbeled base of groin vault; (*b*) arris of true
vault; (*c*) square-edged reveal; (*d*) pointed web.

From Bernay (Fig. 6) in the west, to Reims (Fig. 7) and Vignory in the
east, to Chartres, Auxerre (Fig. 8), and Nevers in the south, ashlar
and frame-and-fill construction dominate. Mixed and loosely coursed
stones constitute walls, and large ashlar blocks surround them at structurally important locations like jambs, corners, and buttresses. Masons
also preferred not to use the regular, rectangular shape of brick-sized
stones for particular functions. Stones with specialized shapes, like
trapezoidal voussoirs, were selected for arches in arcades, windows,

5. Agliate, San Pietro, interior, crypt, eastern end, central and southern aisles; (*a*) pointed web.

and doorways, and classically based moldings – usually a cavetto (*cavet*) or a cavetto with torus – were inserted for imposts and stringcourses.

In northern France, masons overwhelmingly preferred the horizontally extended plan of an ambulatory with radiating chapels in large churches and cathedrals like those at Auxerre, Chartres, Orléans, and Vignory (Fig. 9). In contrast, an ambulatory, let alone radiating chapels, rarely was used in the hundreds of brick-based buildings in southern Europe during the first part of the eleventh century.

6. Bernay, Notre-Dame, interior, nave, southern elevation, string-courses between stories, column, capital, and impost.

7. Reims, Saint-Rémi, exterior, southern transept, chapels, round buttresses, stringcourse, and imposts.

8. Auxerre, Saint-Étienne, interior, crypt, ambulatory, groin vault; (*a*) wide *formeret* stones at the base of the true vault.

At the beginning of the eleventh century, northern French masons also preferred to interrupt horizontally interior walls, vaults, and arcades. In contrast, in the choirs of northern Italian churches, like Sant'-Ambrogio in Milan and San Giovanni at Piobesi Torinese, and in the nave of Catalan churches, like Saint-Martin-du-Canigou, Sant Llorenç de Morunys, and Sant Vicenç at Cardona (Figs. 10, 11), vertical connections are emphasized. In these churches, the underside of a barrel vault continues as a smooth surface into the wall of the nave. Southern masons also preferred to connect square-edged forms on the elevation. Without interruption, *dosserets* vertically continue the square edges of the transverse arches into the square-edged reveals of the compound piers.

In the smallest and largest churches in northern France, and even in Ottonian Germany, masons almost never vaulted the central vessel. In these churches, a pronounced line continues the full length of the nave and separates the wall from the wooden framework overhead. In large northern French churches like those at Bernay (see Fig. 6), Montier-en-Der, Reims, and Vignory, naves are multistoried, and pronounced stringcourse moldings divide the levels and interrupt the ar-

9. Vignory, Saint-Étienne, exterior, chevet.

10. Sant Llorenç de Morunys, abbey church, interior, nave.

11. Cardona, Sant Vicenç, interior, nave, southern wall, detail of first transverse arch and adjacent barrel vault; (*a*) evenly coursed stones in corbeled
portion of vault; (*b*) stones of corbel vault overlap side of transverse arch;
(*c*) irregular stones in true vault; (*d*) stones of true vault continue above extrados
of transverse arch; (e) square stone filling putlog hole.

cades on each story. Not unexpectedly, the creators who designed these
horizontal interruptions also preferred large-scale, projecting sculpted
imposts and capitals at points of articulation.[43]

In northern France, then, builders rejected central-vessel vaulting,
continuous brick-based construction, and square-edged, vertical connections between transverse arches, *dosserets,* and compound piers.
Instead, in the major surviving naves, they made the elevation one
continuous plane from clerestory to pier and used various supports,
projecting moldings, and capitals horizontally to divide this flat surface
into multiple stories.

In contrast, in southern Europe masons translated almost verbatim
into stonework techniques from brick construction in northern Italy.
The nature of rock formations in these regions made it easy for masons trained in Lombard brick techniques to adapt them to stone construction.[44] To build the narthex of Saint-Philibert at Tournus, even
without quarrying, they were able to gather limestones the shape of
brick simply by breaking pieces from the thin sheet rocks that crop out

12. Typical sheet rock in the Mâconnais region (near Blanot).

13. Tournus, Saint-Philibert, exterior, upper narthex, southern clerestory, stones shaped like brick placed in (*a*) diagonal and (*b*) projecting teeth patterns.

14. Tournus, Saint-Philibert, interior, lower narthex, facing west.

of the soil (Fig. 12).[45] Stones that look like homogeneous bricks run in even, uninterrupted courses (Fig. 13) across jambs, around corners, and through vertical bands.[46] Architectural decoration also takes the appearance of brick. Bricks usually repeat a rectangular shape, and therefore, for variety, masons often placed them diagonally – arranging them either lengthwise, to form triangles (Fig. 13a), or, as seen in the Italian context at Novara (see Fig. 3), on their side, to form projecting teeth (Fig. 13b). In decoration on early eleventh-century churches in southern Burgundy, stones rarely are carved into specialized shapes (like cavetto moldings and *doucine* [*cyma recta*] corbels) that reveal an interest in the tradition of Roman ashlar carving.[47]

The inside of the lower Tournus narthex (Fig. 14) has little ashlar masonry and no classically based orders with bases, columns, and capitals.[48] Masons preferred brick-based construction: Socles, neckings, and transverse arches are made from the same type of square-edged, brick-shaped stones that are used in the coursed round piers.[49] They also preferred brick-based articulation: The surface from the underside of each arch continues directly into the round support, without the interruption of an ashlar molding or capital. The next two chapters show that Burgundian masons complemented this construction and articulation, based on brick, with the brick-based structure of the pointed arch and groin vault from Lombardy.

2

The Pointed Arch and Groin Vault in Northern Italy

In Lombardy at the beginning of the eleventh century, masons developed a system of vaulting that was light, flexible, and easy to build. This system of vault construction was used in contemporary architecture throughout southern Europe. In the eleventh and twelfth centuries, these principles continued to influence the structure of major buildings in Burgundy.

In this system, Italian masons used round arches, emphasized the square edges of brick, and integrated the pointed web in groin-vault construction. In aisles and crypts, they usually first laid the framework for the groins with semicircular arcades, *formerets,* and transverse arches; they then corbeled the lower portion of the groin vault; finally they built the upper portion of the web as a true vault. On the side of the web they extended the semicircular segment into a shape that resembles a point.

BRICK GROIN VAULTS IN LOMBARDY

In most important early eleventh-century Lombard churches, the plaster that covers the vaults masks the bricks in the webs. This condition usually makes the study of vault construction impossible. The vaults in the three western aisle bays of the parish church of Santa Maria Maggiore at Lomello provide an important exception because they

15. Lomello, Santa Maria Maggiore, nave, northern aisle, three western bays.

have been left in such a ruined state that the bricks in the webs and cross section of the vaults are completely exposed (Fig. 15).[1]

Corbel-Vault Construction

Two standard techniques of groin construction were used to make the vaults in the side aisles at Lomello. For the base of the vaults, masons used corbel construction (horizontal coursing), and for the webs, they used true-vault construction (nonhorizontal coursing) with temporary centering.

In each bay, on top of the aisle wall, the outside edge of the brick courses forms a semicircular profile. Where the *formerets* have disappeared in the third bay of the northern aisle wall, a section of this profile is still visible (on the right in Fig. 16a). Masons used the top of this rounded wall surface as a platform to project the large, flat bricks of the *formeret* (Fig. 16b). The cantilever of this *formeret* allowed them to build the vault, which rests on the *formeret*, narrower than the width of the aisle. During construction, the *formeret*, nave arcade, and trans-

16. Lomello, Santa Maria Maggiore, nave, northern aisle, third bay, northern wall; (*a*) brick courses forming a semicircular platform for the *formeret;* (*b*) *formeret* made of a double row of bricks.

verse arches – the round-headed arches on the four sides of the vault – provided a platform that could be used to brace the centering for the true vault webs.[2]

From each corner of the bay, masons started to erect the groin web. The profile of the base of the groin (Fig. 17a) resembles the continuous, square-edged profile of the *formerets* adjacent to it (Fig. 17b). At this low point in construction, a true vault is not necessary because the overhang of the web is not sufficient to require centering to lay the stones. Instead, up to approximately 25 percent of the height of the vault, builders laid the stone webs with corbeled construction.[3] Courses extend directly from the aisle wall into the corbeled base of the vault (Figs. 17c, 18c).[4] Above this level, builders switched to true vault construction. They stopped laying vault bricks horizontally, and took advantage of the introduction of centering to begin abruptly laying bricks in a radiating pattern (Figs. 17d, 18d).

Masons began to construct the aisle vaults by corbeling the lowest courses, where two groin webs converge at a single point. But instead of constructing the base of each of the two webs from separate rectangular bricks, they used single, splaying bricks to support both webs

(Fig. 19). As the vault gets higher, the width of each brick increases, making the two adjacent webs one constructive unit (Fig. 19a). The use of these splaying bricks to form the base of two webs works essentially as a *tas-de-charge* (to borrow a Gothic term), which is defined as the lowest courses of a vault or arch, laid horizontally, and bonded into the wall.[5]

In both southern brick-based and northern frame-and-fill construction, the principle of the corbeled *tas-de-charge* was used widely over a century before it was applied to rib-vaulted stone construction.[6] The *tas-de-charge* – especially as built at Lomello, with single bricks that span two webs – offers significant structural benefits. Single blocks that course directly into the wall provide a firm base to spring the true vault.[7] Also, by inserting these corbeled blocks in the lower portion of the vault, masons could start the true vault higher up, and further inside the aisle, than if they had not cantilevered the base of the vault. These mechanisms enable the true-vault span to be narrowed, which in turn reduces the time, labor, and the complicated wooden centering and radiating stones needed to build a true vault.[8] Narrowing the true-vault span also reduces the weight that the radiating stones exert onto the pier and wall.[9]

Placing the corbeled *tas-de-charge* below the true vault achieves another important structural objective by avoiding the problem known as *stress concentration*. A region of high compressive stress occurs at the base of the vault, where the weight of the groin meets the pier and wall. Tensile stress also concentrates at points such as these, building as it does around any abrupt change in section, such as in the radical convergence of a groin web to a point.[10] In the aisles at Lomello, masons lowered the radical sectional shift of the web so that it occurs in the corbeled courses of the wall, and elevated the springing of the real vault above this point of stress. The problem of compressive and tensile stress concentration was thereby sizably reduced. Having less stress with which to contend, they could build lighter, thinner, and less expensive walls, as well as larger and more open spaces.

Italian masons had refined the system of isolated support in the early eleventh century, before the pointed barrel and rib vault were used widely in France. It was primarily in the context of the groin vault that they learned to reduce both kinds of stress concentration and increase the potential for light, space, and delicacy.

17. Lomello, Santa Maria Maggiore, nave, northern aisle, first bay, intersection of western and northern walls; (*a*) springing of the groin web; (*b*) springing of the *formeret;* (*c*) corbeled base of the vault; (*d*) radially laid bricks; (*e*) thin, horizontally laid bricks above *formeret;* (*f*) thick, horizontally laid bricks between *formeret* and crown of the web.

18. Lomello, Santa Maria Maggiore, nave, northern aisle, first bay, western wall; (*c*) corbeled base of the groin vault; (*d*) radially laid bricks; (*e*) thin, horizontally laid bricks above *formeret;* (*f*) thick, horizontally laid bricks between *formeret* and crown of the web.

Pointed Arch in Groin-Vault Construction

The pointed arch, another device with important implications for medieval architecture, also was used in the aisle vaults at Lomello. In the space above the *formerets* and below the radiating stones of the true vault, masons added a row of horizontal filler bricks. In the corners, just below the height where the true vault begins, they started to lay these stretchers (Figs. 17e, 18e) as thin slivers, about a third the height of the *formeret* bricks below them. Toward the peak of the *formeret,* the height of the filler bricks progressively increases (Figs. 17f, 18f) to equal the height of the *formeret* bricks.[11]

The effect, and presumably the purpose, of inserting progressively taller filler blocks above the semicircular *formerets* was to raise the peak of the webs of the groin vault. To support these pointed webs, masons needed to point the top of the structure on which the outside of each web rested. They made up the difference in profile between the pointed vault web and the semicircular *formeret* arch by inserting filler bricks above the center point of the arch.[12]

Pointed webs are an attractive option because they offer structural, constructive, and aesthetic benefits over round-headed webs. The

19. Lomello, Santa Maria Maggiore, nave, northern aisle, first bay, intersection of western and northern walls, corbeled base of the groin vault; (a) splayed brick running between two webs (detail of area shown in Fig. 17).

weight from a pointed web descends at a steeper angle than that from a round-headed web. Weight that descends at a more vertical, as opposed to a more diagonal, angle requires less lateral support, and therefore requires less time, money, and labor to build.[13] A more efficient structure also permits larger openings and thinner walls and supports.

By pointing the web and increasing its angle of descent, masons could narrow the angle the web projects to either side of the groin line (see Figs. 17, 19). In analogy to folding accordion pleats in paper, narrowing the angle of projection of the thin stone webs improves the rigidity of the vault. In addition, masons often reduced the load of the vault by flattening the top of the webs where the groin lines cross. Flattening the crown reduces the lateral thrust and the weight of the vault webbing, allowing thinner supports in the walls and responds on the sides of the vault.[14]

The inherent flexibility of the pointed web offers an important aesthetic benefit over the fixed semicircular web, in that the height of a point in theory can be extended infinitely. By varying the height of pointed webs in groin vaults, masons could equalize an uneven crown line and create a continuous aisle space.

In a rectangular space (such as in the side-aisle bays at Lomello), the diagonal lines that cross in the center are longer than the perpendicular lines that circumscribe them (see Fig. 15). A groin vault creates an uneven crown line when the diagonally intersecting, semicircular groin lines reach a level that is higher than the peak of the shorter adjacent semicircular nave arcades, transverse arches, and *formerets*. Masons could have avoided this problem by making the intersecting diagonal groin lines of circle segments less than semicircular. This arrangement would have depressed the center of the vault to correspond to the height of the smaller adjacent semicircular arches. In northern France at the beginning of the eleventh century, masons almost invariably chose this solution to even the crown line of groin vaults (see "short-segmenting" in the next section).

Southern European masons who built in the brick tradition normally did not use shortened groin segments to depress the diagonal groin lines to the lower height and narrower diameter of the surrounding arches. Instead, they preferred to keep the groin lines relatively steep and straight, flatten the top of the vault, and elevate the peak of the webs on the sides, where they rested on the adjacent arches (see Figs. 4, 5). At Lomello, they rested these webs on gently pointed mounds of filler bricks that are placed above the shorter round nave, *formeret,* and transverse arches (Drawing 1). In certain bays, above the arcade on the side of the nave, the pointed webs rest on the extrados of voussoirs that are longer, and therefore taller, in the middle of the arch than on the sides (see the arcade on the left in Fig. 15).

Early eleventh-century Lombard masons perceived the advantages of the pointed arch in a far different light than later Gothic builders who built pointed stone ribs. For Lombard masons, a positive by-product of pointing groin webs was that it allowed them to keep the surrounding arches – the arcades, *formerets,* and transverse arches – semicircular. By pointing the web, as opposed to the arches, they could improve the structure, even the crown line, and increase light, space, and delicacy – without sacrificing the framework of round-headed construction. The value they placed on round-headed arches probably was significant, because throughout the eleventh century,

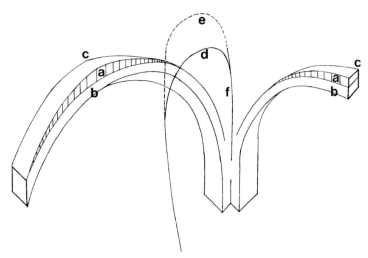

Drawing 1. Typical brick-based groin vault from the early
eleventh century. (*a*) Horizontal fillers are inserted above the (*b*)
brick-shaped voussoirs of the *formeret* and transverse arch and
below the (*c*) pointed outside surface of the web. The (*d*) diagonal
groin is flattened at the top rather than extended into a (*e*)
semicircle, and it is supported by a (*f*) straightened corbel at the
base of the vault.

even in later vaulted buildings with ribs and domes like Sant'Ambrogio
in Milan and Rivolta d'Adda, Lombard masons preferred to build arcades, *formerets,* and transverse arches with a semicircular shape.

From the beginning of the eleventh century, Lombard masons also
adapted the pointed vault and *tas-de-charge* to the shape of brick. They
took advantage of the homogeneous, square-edged quality of bricks to
create continuous vertical reveals that stretch from the bottom of the
pier to the top of the vault. This continuous vertical articulation appears in the side aisles at Lomello, where masons adapted the shape
of the material to the forms and articulation of the vault, wall, and supports (see Fig. 17). The *tas-de-charges*, groin arrises, *formerets*, arcades,
and *dosserets* all have analogous, square-edged vertical reveals. These
squared brick edges continue from the floor to the ceiling, without the
interruption of carved capitals, columns, or moldings.[15]

In summary, masons exploited the aesthetic potential of the *tas-de-
charge* and pointed vault in the context of the round-headed brick arch.
They also used these two devices in ways that made structural and constructive sense. Building a *tas-de-charge* solidified the base and reduced

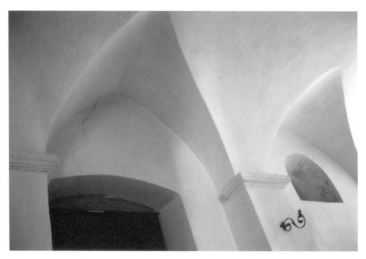

20. Corvey, abbey church, interior, westwork, ground floor, northern wall, pointed webs.

the stress concentrated at the springing of the vault; corbeling the base of the groin narrowed the span of the true vault and minimized the amount of centering required to build it; and pointing the web directed the weight from the vault to the wall more efficiently than in round-headed construction.

Lombard masons almost seamlessly merged the structural and constructional advantages of the corbeled and pointed vault with the articulation and shape of round-headed brick arches. It did not take long for this remarkable synthesis, formulated in the brick architecture of northern Italy, to impact stone building across the southern littoral of Europe.

GROIN VAULTS IN NORTHERN FRANCE AND GERMANY

Before the Romanesque period, Carolingian builders had occasionally used pointed webs. In the crypt of the abbey church at Flavigny and the ground floor of the westwork of the abbey church at Corvey (Fig. 20), there are pointed groin and barrel webs. These devices are used as part of a horizontal articulation, in which moldings, sculpture, and supports interrupt the groin lines.[16] Pronounced and projecting im-

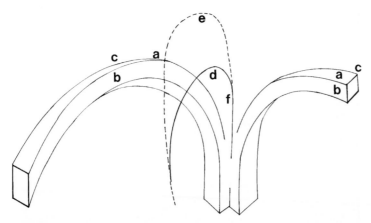

Drawing 2. Typical northern French groin vault from the early eleventh century. (*a*) No horizontal fillers are inserted above the (*b*) ashlar voussoirs of the *formeret* and transverse arch; the (*c*) outside surface of the web is not pointed. The (*d*) diagonal groin is formed from a circle segment rather than extended into a (*e*) full semicircle, and it is supported by a (*f*) straightened corbel at the base of the vault.

posts, above columns, pilasters, and capitals, break the groins at the springing of the vaults. On the sides of these vaults, the pointed webs do not extend directly into continuous, square-edged, vertical reveals.

The contrast is even more striking between the structure and aesthetic of southern First Romanesque architecture and contemporary architecture in northern France. In northern French churches, masons almost never pointed webs or used this structural device as part of a continuous vertical articulation.

It is not as if northern European masons did not face the same problem of uneven groin crown lines as their southern counterparts. Diagonal groin lines – being longer, and therefore taller, than the adjacent semicircular arcades and transverse arches – cause the center of the vault to be higher than the sides. The solution to avoid humped vaults, however, was not to point the webs, make the groin legs as straight as possible, and flatten the peak of the groin lines. Rather, in northern France masons consistently chose to drop the whole vault to the level of the adjacent arches by "short-segmenting" the groin lines. The center section of the groin line usually is kept as close as possible to a pure circle segment, but its length is shortened to less than a semicircle (Drawing 2). Shortening the groin segment effectively lowers the

21. Soissons, Saint-Médard, interior, crypt, lateral hall, groin vault.

height of the webs in relation to the height of the arches beneath the vaults. In most cases these nave and transverse arches are semicircular; where the span between supports is particularly narrow, they are stilted. Keeping arches and groin lines a constant circular shape simplified the construction of centering and the laying of arch and vault stones.

While early eleventh-century northern French and southern European builders had different approaches to construction, structure, and design, they shared the technology of the corbel vault. Below short-segmented groins, northern French masons usually inserted a corbeled base. This combination of short-segmented groins and a corbeled base can be found even in a tenth-century northern French building like the crypt of Saint-Médard at Soissons (Fig. 21). The vault maintains a steep and relatively straight angle in the corbeled section, but at the level of the true vault it abruptly shifts to a short circle segment that continues across the crown.

The cross section of the ruined tribunes in the south aisle of Notre-Dame at Jumièges exposes a similar shift in construction from a corbeled base to a true vault. At about 25 percent of the height of the vault, the horizontal courses at the base of the vault abruptly change to radially laid stones (Fig. 22a). Although northern builders shared the

22. Jumièges, Notre-Dame, nave, southern aisle, tribune, groin vault; cross section showing coursed stones in corbel, (*a*) radially laid stones in true vault, and (*b*) semicircular webs.

corbeling technique with their southern contemporaries, they typically did not accompany this technology with pointed-web construction or continuous vertical articulation. Instead, as seen at Jumièges, short-segmented groins depress the webs to the height of the round-headed arches (Fig. 22b), and a strongly projecting stringcourse molding interrupts the groin lines of the vault.

In the northern aisles, the groin vaults again show a steeply corbeled springing that abruptly switches to a short-segmented groin at about a quarter of the height of the vault (Fig. 23). Shortening the segment of the groin lines across the center of the vault allowed masons to lower the crown without pointing the webs. There is no indication of a pointed web, even in the short span between the colonnette of the nave compound pier and the colonnette of the aisle. Instead, a stilt raises the semicircular transverse arch (Fig. 23a), and a narrow wall makes up for the gap between the springing of the web and the springing of the transverse arch (Fig. 23b). These adjustments allow the profile of the short-segmented groin to extend farther, beyond the narrow, semicircular diameter of the transverse arch.

23. Jumièges, Notre-Dame, nave, interior, northern aisle, groin vault, with (*a*) stilted transverse arch and (*b*) narrow wall at the springing.

In the lower narthex of the abbey church at Saint-Benoît-sur-Loire and in the crypt of the cathedral at Auxerre (Figs. 24, 25; see Fig. 8), masons took a similar approach to creating an even crown line without pointing the webs. In both cases, the base of the vault has a relatively straight and steep corbeled base. An abrupt change occurs where the corbel vault becomes a true vault, as the steep groins become short circle segments. Following the pattern at Jumièges, the builders avoided using pointed webs by maintaining these short-segmented groins over the narrower semicircular transverse arches. To support the short groin segments, they stilted the arches beneath the webs and widened the stones adjacent to the springing of the arches (Fig. 25a; see Fig. 8a).

Elsewhere in northern France, in major early eleventh-century buildings like the crypts of Bayeux, Chartres, Étampes, and Nevers, vaults similarly combine a corbeled springing with short-segmented groins. Webs are almost never pointed, and groins are rarely flattened at the crown. This combination of corbeled and short-segmented vaults also appears widely in early eleventh-century Ottonian architecture. In the vaults of the crypts at Hersfeld and Speyer, for example, corbeled groins begin with a relatively straight and steep profile (Figs. 26a, 27a).

24. Saint-Benoît-sur-Loire, abbey church, interior, narthex, ground floor, groin vault with steeply corbeled base and short-segmented groins.

25. Saint-Benoît-sur-Loire, abbey church, interior, narthex, ground floor; (*a*) narrow wall of stones inserted next to springing of transverse arch.

26. Hersfeld, abbey church, interior, crypt, northern wall, groin vault with (*a*) corbeled base and (*b*) semicircular webs.

At the level where the stones begin to be laid radially, however, the profile of the groins changes to a short circle segment (Fig. 27b). The change permits the webs on the side of the vault to be the same semicircular shape as the *formerets* and transverse arches beneath them (Figs. 26b, 27). It is typical of Ottonian builders that they were able to synthesize Roman, Carolingian, northern, and southern techniques. Occasionally, as in the vaults on the eastern and western walls of the crypt at Hersfeld, they introduced pointed webs alongside shortsegmented vaults.[17]

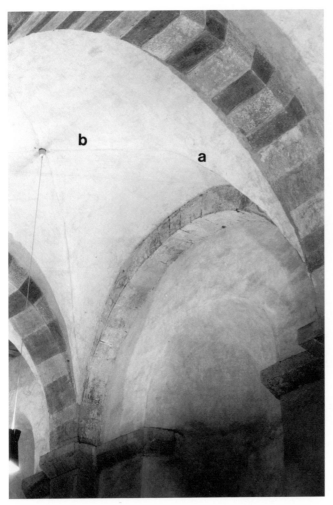

27. Speyer, cathedral, interior, hall crypt, southern transept,
groin vault with (*a*) corbeled base, (*b*) short-segmented
groins, and semicircular webs.

STONE GROIN VAULTS IN LOMBARDY AND THE PIEDMONT

In the early eleventh century, masons who built brick vaults spread
their knowledge of construction, structure, and design throughout the
territory where the Franco-Provençal dialect was spoken. Italian masons either traveled to Burgundy or transmitted their brick techniques
to masons who built stone architecture in this area of France.

Another possibility is that masons in France did not make the translation from brick to stone themselves but learned brick techniques

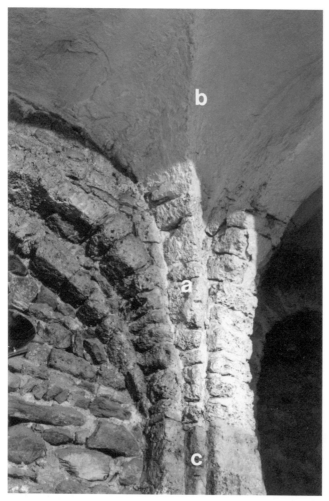

28. Aosta, cathedral, interior, crypt, northern wall; (*a*) corbeled base of groin vault; (*b*) arris of true vault; (*c*) square-
edged reveal.

from Italian stone structures. Where stone is available in northern Italy,
masons occasionally built stone architecture using brick techniques.
Oval river-bed stones usually are used, or, less often, as in the region
of Lake Como and the Valley of Aosta, small rectangular rocks. Regard-
less of the type and source of the stones that they employed, however,
these Italian masons normally treated stones as bricks. They selected
small, uniformly shaped stones, laid them in continuous horizontal
courses, and applied structural techniques associated with brick building. These stones also are articulated in the manner of actual bricks.
Analogous square-edged reveals line the stone walls and connect di-

29. Aime, Saint-Martin, interior, choir, northern wall; (*a*) pointed web.

rectly to the vault, often without horizontal capitals or continuous moldings.

The crypts at Aosta cathedral and San Michele at Oleggio are built with small, regular, horizontal stones (Fig. 28; see Fig. 4). In the supports, these stones form analogous square-edged reveals that connect – without the interruption of imposts or moldings –- with groins, *formerets,* and transverse arches.[18]

Below the level of the true vault, masons coursed the stones of the wall and piers into a corbel vault. They took advantage of the easily laid courses in corbel construction to extend the lower section of the groin web into a steep vertical angle (Fig. 28a; see Fig. 4a).[19] At the base of the webs, the square-edged reveals (Fig. 28c; see Fig. 4c) are analogous to the continuous orders of the *formerets* and transverse arches that descend next to them.[20] At a point 25 percent of the height of the vault, where gravity requires centering to support the radiating stones of a true vault, the steep and straight angle of the groins abruptly shifts to a slightly more horizontal direction (Fig. 28b; see Fig. 4b) and flattens further at the crown of the vault.[21]

Pointed webs usually are used in these kinds of groin. (In the crypt at Oleggio and in the choir at Aime, just across the Italian border, brick-shaped stones replace bricks in the pointed webs [Fig. 29a; see Fig. 4d].)[22] Especially in irregular bays, such as in the trapezoidal bays next to the curved apse wall in the crypt of San Pietro at Agliate, the difference in the length – and thus usually the height – of the *formerets,* transverse arches, and groin lines causes the crown of the webs to vary between arches (see Fig. 5a).[23] To even the crown line, masons pointed the webs, allowing the webs to reach the height of the longer and higher diagonal groin lines.[24]

Centering for Groin Vaults

Did the type of wooden centering that was needed to build the true vault affect the construction, structure, and design of the groin vault? It almost surely did. In the crypts at Oleggio and Agliate (see Figs. 4, 5), as in many other groin-vaulted Lombard structures, a change occurs where the corbel vault becomes a true vault. As the groin lines abruptly shift to a slightly more horizontal direction, the shape of the webs become noticeably more irregular.

One reason comes to mind as to why masons made the top part of the web in each bay a different irregular shape. They could not reuse slats and cleats of standardized sizes and shapes to build a multifaceted vault with a continuously changing profile in a tight and irregular space. Instead, they needed to develop techniques that would allow them to maneuver, with flexibility, speed, and minimal cost, within these narrow and irregular confines. It is widely assumed that masons erected centering on scaffolding built from the ground, on beams stretching across the aisle, or on a temporary structure suspended from transverse arches and *formerets.*

It is further surmised that sometimes masons covered the lag boards on the centering with an indeterminate rough fill (one can only speculate on material that was malleable enough to be shaped to an irregular outline but dense enough not to sag under weight). They then set the true-vault portion of the vault on this ephemeral framework.[25] Masons may very well have used this fill method, but there is little if any evidence to prove it. The irregular fill, if it existed, did not leave a trace on the mortar that oozed between the web stones onto the underside of the vault.

In contrast, the impressions of short lag boards often remain in the mortar beneath groin vaults. Two examples of these impressions left by lag boards survive in Alpine churches next to the Italian border. In the

30. Saint-Jean-de-Maurienne, cathedral, interior, crypt, springing of groin vault; (*a*) impressions left by lag boards above extrados of *formeret.*

groin vaults in the crypt of the cathedral of Saint-Jean-de-Maurienne and in the transept apse of Saint-Martin at Aime, the marks left by the ends of lag boards show that masons laid them directly on top of the extrados of the *formerets* and transverse arches (Figs. 30a, 31a; Drawing 3). Centering would have been necessary to support these small irregular boards, but no space remains to insert beams between the lag boards and the top of the arch stones.

In these instances, masons would have needed to build an independent centering. A freestanding wooden structure or even centering that

31. Aime, Saint-Martin, interior, southern transept, apse, arcade; (*a*) impressions left by lag boards above extrados of arch.

rested on a suspended beam would have required a large amount of time, expertise, and timber to build. I am sure in many cases this was the standard practice. A less costly and more efficient solution would have been to rest the wooden framework directly against the sides of the voussoirs.[26] This system for supporting lag boards would have been structurally efficient, because the more the stones of the vault push down on the centering, the more these wooden beams would flex and attach themselves into the sides of the stone arches. This system of wooden formwork that rests between sides of stone arches also would have been efficient from the point of view of construction. Because the scaffolding rests between arches and not on top of them, once the arch and vault stones dry, masons could easily knock down the timbers and reuse them without destabilizing the stone structure.[27]

CONCLUSION

The standard definition of a groin vault is a vault that results from the intersection of two equal barrel vaults. This simple, regular, and geometric definition, based on a Roman model, does not adequately de-

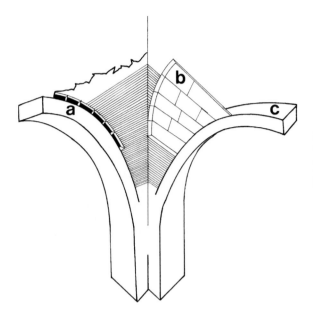

Drawing 3. (*a*) Impressions in vault mortar left by (*b*) lag boards placed above the (*c*) extrados of the *formeret* and transverse arch.

scribe the brick-based groin vaults that masons built at the turn of the eleventh century in northern Italy. This standard description mentions neither the shifting shapes within these groins – due to the constructive change from a steep corbel vault to a true vault with a flattened peak – or the irregular warping of true-vault webs – due to the use of temporary centering and nonstandardized lag boards in the upper portion of the vault. It also does not take into account the pointing of the web – used to compensate for the discrepancy in height between diagonal groin lines and the smaller semicircular *formerets* and transverse arches beneath the groin webs. Instead, the definition concentrates on the geometric shape of the vault, and it establishes a standard based on the intersection of two vaults of another type (the barrel vault).[28]

Practically speaking, however, in the brick-based vaults of Italy, masons built groin lines and their accompanying pointed webs with wobbly shapes. They built these vaults in two phases and used a distinctive construction in each: They used horizontal courses from the wall to build the corbel vault, and temporary wooden scaffolding to lay the radially laid bricks of the pointed true vault. The uneven and changing character of the groin vault, then, was determined less by the geometry of hypothetically converging barrel vaults than by the mundane considerations of building. Masons looked for ways, in keeping with a continuous vertical aesthetic, to improve the structure of the vault, even the crown line, and reduce materiel and labor. To satisfy these requirements, in one vault they combined two different structures, a corbeled base and pointed webs, to achieve minimal thrust and a narrow true-vault span.

CHAPTER

3

The Pointed Arch and Groin Vault at the Beginning of the Eleventh Century in Burgundy

 At the beginning of the eleventh century, the regions of northern Italy and southern Burgundy were linked by language, geography, and the brick technique of building. Although the masons in these regions shared a common heritage, they preferred different types of structure. In Italy, they usually followed the pattern of Early Christian builders, who made unvaulted naves with simple monolithic supports. In southern Burgundy, they preferred vaulted naves, large round piers, and geometric shapes at points of articulation.[1]

TOURNUS LOWER NARTHEX

The lower narthex of Saint-Philibert at Tournus is one of the largest early eleventh-century structures in France (Fig. 32; see Fig. 14).[2] The central vessel is covered with square groin vaults and the two aisles with transverse barrel vaults. Unevenly finished stones the shape of small bricks are used for almost every part of the interior, including the walls, transverse arches, wall arcades, round piers, and even the socles and neckings of the piers

To build the groin vaults in the lower narthex, masons followed the Italian method of corbeled and pointed-web construction. In each bay, they first constructed the *formerets* and transverse arches and then corbeled the lower courses of the groin vault. One can deduce that the

49

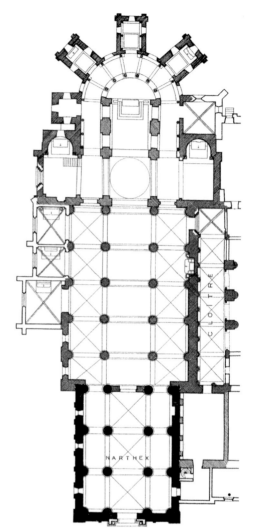

32. Tournus, Saint-Philibert, plan (after Maurice Berry, 1955).

lower portion of the groin is corbeled from the relative position of the stones in the vault in relation to the stones in the *formeret* and transverse arches. The stones in the lower, corbeled portion of the vault, are in front of, and therefore came after, the stones in the arches behind them (Fig. 33a). At this level of the groin web, then, the extrados of the arches could not have been used to lay lag boards for a true vault.

As in Italian vaults, the corbeled base is straighter and steeper than the true vault above it. At about 25 percent of the height of the groin, the previously built *formerets* and transverse arches could have been

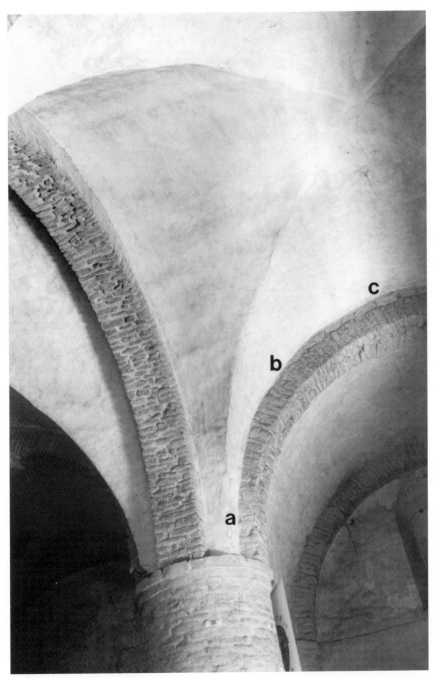

33. Tournus, Saint-Philibert, interior, lower narthex, western bay, central and northern aisles; (*a*) corbel vault, overlapping the face of arch; (*b*) web of true vault resting above the extrados of the arch; (*c*) pointed groin web.

used to brace the wooden centering and lag boards for the true vault. At this level, the vault reflects these changes in construction, because it abruptly alters its position in relation to the arches. The web rests above the extrados, instead of in front of the face of the voussoirs (Fig. 33b); and the groin lines become more horizontal and irregular than in the corbel vault below.[3] Even these true-vault groin lines, however, are straighter than they would be in a typical short-segmented northern groin vault. At the peak of the vault, the angle of the groin lines flattens.

In the lower narthex at Tournus, the pointed lateral webs of the groin vaults serve the same purpose as the pointed groin-vault webs at Lomello (Figs. 33c, 34). Given the geometry of a square bay (see Fig. 32), the line of the diagonal groins is longer, and therefore higher, than the semicircle of the perpendicular transverse arches adjacent to it. To compensate for this difference in size, masons made the groin webs taller on the sides, by pointing the webs where they descend to meet the lower transverse arches.

In the lower narthex at Tournus, masons could easily have stilted the transverse arches, as is the case in the aisles of the later nave and upper narthex. This extra length would have elevated the crown of the webs on the sides of the vault to reach the height of the webs at the crossing of the groin lines. For good structural reasons, however, they chose not to raise the webs by stilting the arches.

In the aisles adjacent to the main vessel, masons rested the edges of the lateral barrel vaults on transverse arches so low that the arches spring below the necking of the piers (see Fig. 14). Every inch gained in this manner by lowering the semicircular barrel vaults could be used to narrow the mass where the webs intersect at the springing of the vaults. Reducing the bulk of the masonry at this springing also allows them to narrow the width of the transverse arch that is needed to support it. A narrower transverse arch, in turn, saves materials, time, and labor, and decreases the heaviness of the structure.

In the aisles, the major advantage of lowering the transverse arches comes from the role they play in buttressing the weight from the groin vaults in the central vessel and transferring it to the outside walls.[4] Groin vaults probably were selected for this location because they brought aesthetic benefits: Groin vaults, with point support and pointed webs, allow light and space from the side aisles freely to enter the

34. Tournus, Saint-Philibert, interior, lower narthex, central bay, detail of southern arcade; (*a*) stones in the shape of bricks, placed horizontally between the extrados of the arcade and the web of the groin vault.

central bays, where there is no clerestory or raised elevation. The structural downside of this type of groin vault is that it produces narrowly focused, stressful points of weight that have to be supported. In the central vessel, above each freestanding round pier, the weight from two converging groin webs passes, at a relatively vertical angle, from above the pier necking to below the pier necking in the side aisle (see Figs. 14, 32, 33). To stabilize this converging and steeply descending weight, masons had to find a way, at the lowest possible level, to buttress the freestanding pier and transfer the thrust from the central vault to the outside wall.

To accomplish these goals, they lowered the springing of each transverse barrel vault below the level of the necking of the adjacent freestanding pier. Beneath this springing, they also dropped the level of the transverse arch that buttresses the freestanding pier. At first glance, the low height of the springing of the transverse barrel vault and transverse arch seems to do nothing but interrupt the interior space by blocking the line of sight down the aisle. Moreover, the transverse arch, for no good reason, seems to interrupt the pier by severing its necking and colliding into its side. In fact, however, the transverse barrel allows light and space to penetrate laterally into the central vessel; and the low height of the transverse arch provides outstanding support for the steeply descending weight from the groin vault.[5]

A price had to be paid, however, to receive the structural benefits of springing barrel vaults at a low level. Once masons decided not to stilt the semicircular barrels but, instead, to drop the webs and transverse arches as low as possible below the pier necking, they were left with little choice for the size of the semicircular longitudinal arcade. They had to make the circumference of the extrados of these arcades the same dimension as the circumference of the semicircular barrel vaults, whose webs the arcade arches also support.

This relationship, in which the circumference of the semicircular barrel vaults determines the circumference of the semicircular arches in the adjacent arcade, did not pose a problem of aesthetics or construction in the aisles. The problem came in the adjacent central vessel, where the lateral webs of the groin vaults rest on the same longitudinal semicircular arches as the barrel vaults in the aisles (see Fig. 33). The crown where these groin lines cross is substantially higher than the top of the extrados of the longitudinal arcades; therefore, in order to keep the groin webs from drooping where they rest on the arcades, masons had to point the lateral web of the vaults. At Tournus, then, it is in the context of building groin webs – specifically, to make their height align with the crown of the groin – and not in the context of building barrel vaults, transverse arches, or groin lines, that masons introduced the point in vault construction.[6] In a similar context in the brick church at Lomello, Lombard masons introduced a point to heighten the webs in relation to the crown of the groin.

In the brick construction at Lomello, masons prepared to lay the pointed groin webs by inserting progressively larger brick slivers above the semicircular *formerets*. In the first two bays at Tournus, progressively larger filler stones also run between the extrados of the semicircular arches and the peak of the groin webs (see Figs. 33c, 34a). These filler stones serve two objectives, both related to construction. By keeping the longitudinal arches semicircular – and thus lower than the pointed webs of the central-vessel groins – masons could use these arches to support the intentionally depressed, semicircular barrels in the aisles. It was only on the other side of the arcades – the side of the central vessel – that they inserted the row of progressively larger filler stones above the arches. This additional construction serves a second purpose, which is to allow the same round-headed, longitudinal arches to support the higher, pointed groin webs in the central vessel (see Fig. 33).[7]

The close parallels between the groin vaults at Tournus and Lomello show that masons in Burgundy had mastered the most complicated brick techniques of vaulting. Despite sharing a similar approach to structure, however, masons on opposite sides of the Alps preferred different types of buildings. Italian masons clearly preferred wooden-ceiling basilicas: They relegated barrels to small, low choirs, and assigned groin vaults a subsidiary role in the aisles and crypts.

In contrast, in important churches in Burgundy, the masons who used brick techniques usually preferred an entirely vaulted structure. Pointed groin webs are used in complex, fully vaulted systems that include an important role for the barrel vault. In these systems, masons fully integrated the barrel and groin vaults, and, from all indications, did not see one type of vault as an evolutionary improvement over the other.[8] Rather, in buildings like the lower narthex at Tournus, they utilized the unique structural, constructional, and aesthetic properties of each vault type to reinforce the benefits and reduce the deficits of the other. At Tournus, they succeeded in combining the barrel and groin vault to create an open, lighted, fully vaulted central space.[9]

SAINT-MARTIN AT CHAPAIZE

A short distance from Tournus, the brick-based parish church of Saint-Martin at Chapaize again combines barrel and groin vaults (Fig. 35).[10] Traces of the original round-headed barrel vault survive at each end of the central vessel, and many of the original groin vaults still cover the aisles. Masons used the standard techniques of brick vault construction to build these groin vaults: First they erected the arcades, *formerets*, and transverse arches, and built a corbeled base to approximately 25 percent of the height of the vault (Fig. 36a). Unlike in the lower narthex at Tournus, however, where the stones in the corbeled base overlap the sides of the preexisting arches, in the western bays of the aisle at Chapaize, the stones in the corbeled groin web course with the stones in the springing of the adjacent arches (Figs. 36b, 37b). The corbeled stones in the base of the groin, therefore, must have been built

35. Chapaize, Saint-Martin, interior, nave, central vessel, southern wall (author's photo from restoration file, Caisse Nationale des Monuments Historiques).

at the same time, and as part of, the nave and aisle walls. Indeed, based on the evidence of the arcade arch in the third southern bay, masons went even farther and coursed the stones in the corbeled groin into a massive building platform at the bottom of the nave elevation. In this structure, horizontally coursed stones from the corbeled aisle web extend not only into the springing of the arcade arch (Fig. 38a) but also into the lower beds of the rounded nave responds (Fig. 38b).

Above the corbeled base, the overhang of the web required the masons to use centering to build the webs as a true groin vault. Evidence of this change in construction can be seen in the radially laid stones

36. Chapaize, Saint-Martin, interior, nave, southern aisle, western bay, *formeret* and groin web; (*a*) corbel vault; (*b*) coursed stones between web and *formeret*; (*c*) radial stones of true web rest above the extrados of *formeret*.

37. Chapaize, Saint-Martin, interior, nave, northern aisle, western bay, *formeret*, arcade, and groin web; (*b*) coursed stones between web and *formeret*; (*c*) pointed groin web and horizontally laid stones in the shape of brick above extrados of the arch.

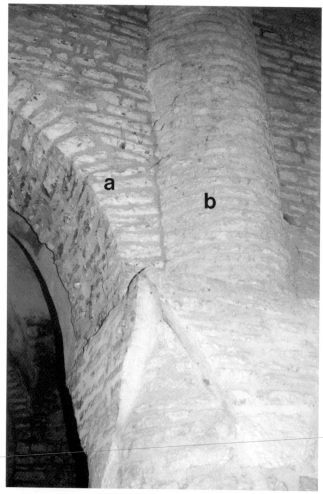

38. Chapaize, Saint-Martin, interior, nave, third southern bay, intersection of respond, arcade, and impost; (*a*) stones in the springing of the arch course with (*b*) stones at the base of the respond.

in the webs of the true vault. Above the corbel vault, the stones no longer course with the arch but instead rest above the voussoirs and filler stones of the arch (see Fig. 36c). In the true vault, the groins remain relatively straight, although they flatten at the peak of the crossing. To keep the webs from drooping on the sides, masons pointed the sides of the webs. To support these pointed webs, toward the apex of the *formerets,* nave arcade, and transverse arches, they inserted progressively larger stones in the shape of brick (see Fig. 37c).[11]

39. Chapaize, Saint-Martin, interior, nave, southern aisle, third freestanding pier.

To narrow the span of the true vault, masons corbeled the base of the vault. They further narrowed the span of the true vault by projecting a trapezoidal pier necking below the corbeled base (Fig. 39). In most important, early eleventh-century, brick-based buildings in the region of Cluny, the top of round piers is a double square-edged round necking. Examples of this type of pier necking can be found in the churches at Combertault, Saint-Hymetière, and Tournus (see Fig. 14).[12] The church at Chapaize also has round piers, but they are capped differently, with four trapezoidal imposts: One faces the nave (see Fig. 38), one faces the aisle (Fig. 39), and one faces each direction of the arcade (see Fig 35). In the greater Burgundy region, this type of trapezoidal pier necking repeats in the brick-based choir of Gigny, nave of Saint-Mesmin, and *dortoir* of Saint-Bénigne of Dijon.[13]

The shape of the trapezoidal necking, which is wider at the top than at the bottom, allows the span of the true vault to be narrowed while preserving the maximum space between the freestanding piers and the aisle walls. At the bottom of the necking, masons used the tapered base of the trapezoid to funnel the wide, projecting necking directly into the round pier; an ashlar block frequently strengthens the point where the necking joins the pier (see Fig. 39). In the restricted space of the aisle, the round pier is an ideal support because it occupies less space than a rectangular or compound pier. Compared with a round pier, a compound pier has the advantage of allowing the continuous orders from the arches and groin lines to connect directly and continuously to the base of the pier. An example of this vertically continuous articulation can be seen in the side aisle of Sant Viçenc at Cardona (Fig. 40). The disadvantage of the compound pier is that in this support the

40. Cardona, Sant Vicenç, interior, nave, southern aisle, continuous orders of freestanding piers and wall responds.

41. Chapaize, Saint-Martin, interior, nave, southern wall, westernmost arcade, intersection of aisle groin vault and impost with nave arcade, impost, and respond.

orders from the vault and arches project horizontally into the space of the aisle, and constrict the narrow space in this passage. In the region of Burgundy, masons preferred narrow-aisle plans, and to help relieve these tight spaces used the round pier as the standard type of support in early Romanesque churches.

In the central vessel at Chapaize, the trapezoidal imposts of the arcade piers cannot connect directly with the barrel vault, because the vault springs at the level of the clerestory, high above the nave arcade (see Fig. 35). Even on the arcade level, however, the projecting ends of the trapezoidal necking do not connect with any part of the nave elevation. Instead, a large void is left where the tips, *dosseret,* and springing of the arcades come together (on the right in Fig. 41). Masons formed the trapezoidal impost, half-cylindrical respond, and the rectangular arcade soffit into distinct geometrical forms, and they separated these shapes by large areas of space. At eye level, this assemblage of shapes that projects like abstract sculpture punctuates the flat elevation of the nave (see Fig. 35).

This unusual articulation appears in other Burgundian brick-based buildings at the beginning of the eleventh century. At the intersection of the wall and arcade in the lower narthex at Tournus, the groin web, transverse arch, and double round necking are spatially separate, geometric units (see Fig. 33). At both Chapaize and Tournus, then, masons followed the Italian tradition by using brick-shaped stones with squared edges, but they arranged these stones into isolated and juxtaposed geometric parts, something Italian masons never did.[14]

In thinking about the pier necking, masons had to keep in mind structural and constructive, as well as aesthetic, considerations. At Chapaize, on the side of the piers facing the aisles, just as on the side of the piers facing the nave, the pier necking extends into a trapezoidal shape (see Figs. 39, 41). In this location on the aisle, however, masons needed to use the necking as a platform from which to spring the transverse arch and corbel the base of the groin vault. They extended the pier into a trapezoid – but without leaving a void above it, as they had done on the side of the pier facing the central vessel. The horizontal courses from the trapezoidal necking simply continue directly into the arches and corbeled webs of the vault. This technique enabled masons to build rapidly and efficiently, because every inch they projected the trapezoid from the pier into the space of the aisle, they could use to narrow the span of the centering and vault. Adjacent to the facade, in the westernmost bay of the southern aisle, they even took the extra step of corbeling the springing of the groin vault beyond the projecting tip of the trapezoidal necking (see Fig. 41). This cantilever allowed the span of the vault to be reduced an extra few inches beyond those gained by projecting the tip of the necking.

In the lower narthex at Tournus, the same principle was used to make the diameter of the centering for the arches and vault as short as possible. At the top of the pier, masons projected a double-stepped, square-edged round necking. On the outside edge of this projecting molding, they rested the corbel vault and the wooden centering and slats for the *formerets* and transverse arches. The extra thickness of the necking allows the springing of the vault and arches to be cantilevered beyond the edge of the pier. This system of corbeled necking at Chapaize and Tournus also permits the maximum space between round piers and the minimum span between arches and vault.[15]

CONCLUSION

At the turn of the eleventh century in southern Burgundy, masons made important new contributions to the structure, construction, and aesthetics of brick-based architecture. In the churches at Tournus and Chapaize, masons built round arches, corbel vaults, and pointed, true-groin vaults in the Italian manner. They also combined this approach with a local preference for complex vaults, round piers, juxtaposed parts, and uniquely corbeled pier neckings.

Southern Burgundian masons used groin and barrel vaults in various combinations to maximize structural efficiency and visual effects. The ground floor of the double-story Tournus narthex is too low to accommodate a longitudinal barrel vault in the central vessel. Instead of reducing the size of the second-story nave by raising the height of the first-story elevation, masons increased the lateral openings between the first-story central and side aisles. For this purpose, in the central vessel they selected groin vaults that left a small footprint where the webs narrow into points above the piers. These groin vaults open a wide, horizontal vista between the central vessel and aisles. They also used transverse barrel vaults in the aisles. The continuous high crown of these vaults allows light and space to enter directly below the pointed groin webs in the central vessel. Masons combined the structural and aesthetic advantages of each vault type – the transverse buttressing and uninterrupted crown line of a barrel with the point support and 360-degree opening of a groin – to exploit the plan and elevation of the lower narthex.

The nave of Chapaize also uses groins and barrels, but different circumstances suggested a different combination of these vaults than in the narthex at Tournus. The lack of a story above ground level meant that masons could extend the central vessel into a barrel vault. This type of structure allowed them to accent the height of the nave and the continuity of the vault with the nave elevation. In the aisles they took advantage of the properties of groin vaults. This type of structure, in conjunction with round piers and corbeled imposts, allowed them to minimize the labor and construction of the vault and arches, and also maximized the light and space in this narrow passage.

In southern Burgundy at the beginning of the eleventh century, masons combined barrel and groin vaults in brick-based architecture. Evidence from the principal monuments gives little indication that they considered one of these vault types to be structurally more efficient or aesthetically more advanced than the other. Instead, the evidence shows that they used different combinations of these vaults to meet specific structural, constructional, and visual objectives.

4

The Pointed Arch and Groin Vault in Burgundy at the End of the Eleventh Century

During the eleventh century, in the region of southern Burgundy masons improved the structure and expanded the range of architecture. In buildings like the small chapel at Berzé-la-Ville and the enormous abbey church at Cluny, they exploited the earlier brick system of corbeled relieving arches to support larger and more complicated barrel vaults.[1] They also took advantage of this improved structure to expose the wall as a series of separate, delicate planes, and to open the central space.[2] Space was opened vertically through high, narrow, and pointed barrel vaults, and horizontally through wide and high aisle arcades.

Masons also refined the skeletal, point-support system that is basic to groin vaulting in First Romanesque architecture. Ashlar was introduced at points of support, and a new scale of classicism and sculptural carving was added to an architecture largely devoid of individual stone decoration. In a building like Cluny III, masons used this sophisticated combination of vaults and supports to create thin, penetrated walls and to open high and wide spaces. They combined the Lombard tradition of construction with local building preferences to produce an astonishingly new architecture.

42. Farges, Saint-Barthélemy, interior, nave, southern aisle.

FARGES

Just a few miles west of Tournus, the small parish church of Saint-Barthélemy at Farges shows the changes to brick-based construction in southern Burgundy (Fig. 42).[3] Masons used the round pier and round necking, standard in the region for almost a century, but they substantially altered them by narrowing the proportions of the pier, chamfering the bottom edge of the necking, and increasing the stone size in the piers and arches.

Masons also altered the traditional shape and structure of brick groin vaults. They began, once again, by using Italian brick vault con-

43. Le Puley, priory church, interior, nave, northern aisle, third bay, detail of wall, vault, and transverse arches; (*a*) brick-shaped stones of original transverse arch; (*b*) springing of original *formeret;* (*c*) traces of original *formeret;* (*d*) replacement *formeret;* (*e*) pointed ashlar of later transverse arch.

struction as the foundation of their approach. In the Italian manner, they combined corbel and true vaults; straightened and flattened the true-vault groins; and evened the crown line by pointing the webs. A lightweight, temporary scaffolding presumably also was used to produce uneven arris lines.

They also changed the structure and construction of barrel and groin vaults, and even merged the characteristics of these two vault types. The use of transverse barrel vaults in the side aisles was adopted from the lower narthex at Tournus, but they improved the construction and structure of these vaults to allow for maximum height and light above the transverse arch. Pointed webs "break" the sides of the lateral barrels and make the vaults sturdier, more structurally efficient, and easier to build than at Tournus.[4]

Changes in vaulting technology occurred even within one building, the ruined priory church at Le Puley. In the eastern bays of the northern aisle, a transverse arch of brick-shaped stones (Fig. 43a) originally sprang at the same level as the adjacent *formeret* on the wall (Fig. 43b).

This original *formeret* no longer exists, but the outline of its stones survives as a semicircular suture (Fig. 43c). This curved suture, and an analogous one in the wall of the preceding bay, still are visible above the aisle window, a few feet below the later *formeret* (Fig. 43d).

The masons had prepared to build vaults in the traditional brick manner, by corbeling the groin webs at the level of the springing of the round-headed transverse arches.[5] Once it was time to vault the aisle, however, they had learned to adapt ashlar to the construction of transverse arches (Fig. 43e). They made the arches in the two western bays structurally more stable and efficient than the arch in the eastern bay by building them with large, trapezoidal voussoirs and pointing the intrados and extrados.

Once the decision was made to raise, reinforce, and point the transverse arches, a number of important changes could be made to the vaults and the *formerets,* on which they rested. Masons could raise the height of the *formerets* (Fig. 43d), shorten their circumference, and reduce the corbel at the base of the vaults. They could also spring the true vaults higher and flatten the profile of their webs.

In southern Burgundy throughout the eleventh century, masons depended upon the corbel at the base of the groin vault to narrow the span of the true vault. They also used this corbel leg aesthetically, as Italians had often used square-edged brick reveals, to make the transition between the vault and support. This device connects the diagonal, creased web lines of the groin vault directly to the vertical, square-edged responds of the wall and pier. This treatment can be found at the beginning of the eleventh century in the chevet of the abbey church at Le Villars, and at the end of the eleventh century in the aisle of the abbey church at Saint-Hippolyte (Fig. 44), where masons extended the corbel into a reveal at the base of the groin vault.

By the end of the century, the use of ashlar on a wide scale gradually changed the pattern of building with brick-shaped stones and square-edged reveals. Even at Farges, which is built with brick-based walls and local brick building types, like the round pier and barrel vault, ashlar framing stones dominate structurally important elements, like the transverse arch (Fig. 45). As masons integrated these large blocks with traditional brick-vaulting techniques, they made adjustments, both large and small, to the normal way of thinking about building. The more they emphasized the framing elements, and distin-

44. Saint-Hippolyte, abbey church, interior, nave, southern aisle, third bay, detail of ruined groin vault.

guished them from the brick-shaped wall fill, the more they departed from the southern First Romanesque tradition of homogeneous, brick courses and vertically continuous, square-edged reveals.

Masons modified the brick techniques of groin vaulting to take advantage of the individual shapes and particular strengths of ashlar. Trapezoidal ashlar voussoirs provide a more secure vault framework than small, brick-shaped arch stones. They took advantage of these specially cut, large framing stones to rethink the construction, position, and shape of the web.

At Farges, the voussoirs of the arcade and transverse arches are tall and wide ashlar blocks, which means that in the corners, where these arches intersect, the extrados converges well above the intrados of the arches (Fig. 45a). By increasing the height of the intersecting extrados of the arcade and transverse arches, masons could lay the vault webs at a much higher level than if they had used smaller, brick-shaped stones as voussoirs. In particular, they could begin the complex and costly true vault at a higher level than before. Most of these stones course radially, as in a fan, over the top of the transverse arch (Fig. 45b). Masons diminished the corbel portion of the vault as well, reducing these horizontally coursed stones to about five beds at the base of the web (Fig. 45c). They also took advantage of the high springing of the vault to flatten the top of the webs (Fig. 45d). In this case, the weight disperses so evenly that it acts almost like a dead load. A flat-top web exerts less diagonal thrust than one with a semicircular profile, and requires thinner walls to support it.[6]

Asymmetrical Webs

The ashlar frame of the arches also was used to modify the shape and improve the performance of the true vault. At Farges, masons started by using the traditional brick method of inserting stretchers between the transverse arch and vault web (Fig. 45e). The miniature diaphragm arch created by these flat stones raises the crown of the webs above the height of the transverse arches.

Above this level, the brick-shaped stones in the webs are modified to take advantage of the ashlar stones in the arches. At the inside corners of the aisle vaults (on the side next to the nave) at the base of the vault, masons converged large ashlar voussoirs from the arcades and transverse arches. Less space remains for the web to descend between the arcade and transverse arch on the inside of the aisle (Fig. 45a) than between the transverse arch and the wall on the outside, where no wall arcade exists (Fig. 45f). With less space to descend, the bottom of the web remains higher, and the width of the web narrower, on the inside than on the outside of the bay.

An asymmetrical vault offers structural advantages over a symmetrical vault. A higher web on the inside than on the outside allows the weight from the central barrel to descend at a more vertical angle through the aisle vault to the outside wall. A more efficient web angle also causes less stress on the freestanding piers and requires a thinner wall and buttresses on the exterior to absorb the weight of the vault.

45. Farges, Saint-Barthélemy, interior, nave, southern aisle, third bay, detail of arcade, transverse arch, and broken barrel vault; (*a*) intersection of ashlar arcade and transverse arch; (*b*) radially laid brick-shaped stones of true vault; (*c*) coursed brick-shaped stones of corbel vault; (*d*) flattened web; (*e*) horizontally placed brick-shaped stones above the extrados of transverse arch; (*f*) low springing of outside web.

Earlier masons, who used more uniform brick-based masonry, had also recognized the principle of asymmetrical webbing and the structural advantages it affords. During the first third of the eleventh century, in the nave of Saint-Philibert at Tournus, masons had made walls, arches, and neckings of brick-shaped stones (Fig. 46).[7] In each aisle bay, the nave arcade (Fig. 46a) and the two adjacent transverse arches (Fig. 46b) are stilted. These raised arches are used to elevate the three groin webs, closest to the central nave, that rest on them. A high groin vault allows the weight from the base of the diaphragm arch in the central vessel to pass directly to the vault webs in the side aisle. Stilting these arches also allows the crown line of the webs, which passes above the narrow transverse arches, to reach the same height as the longer groin lines, which cross in the middle of each bay.

46. Tournus, Saint-Philibert, interior, nave, southern aisle, vaults; (*a*) stilted springing of arcade; (*b*) stilted springing of transverse arch.

In each aisle bay, the fourth arch, the *formeret,* is not stilted to match the height of the arcade and transverse arches. Instead, it remains a semicircle (Fig. 47a). Keeping the wall arcade a half-round shape had an important consequence, because it meant that the outside web (Fig. 47b) could be lowered to the height of this unstilted arch, upon which it rested. Once the builders made the outside web lower than the in-side webs, they could channel the vault weight more vertically, and thus more efficiently, than if all the webs had been the same height.

In the aisles at Tournus, the structure is complicated by added weight from the transverse barrels and diaphragm arches that descends directly onto the transverse arches and vaults. Masons used the asym-metry of the outside webs to pass the weight from the central vessel to the attached piers and thick panels on the exterior wall. With this weight effectively directed to isolated exterior supports, they could narrow and elongate the freestanding piers as well as thin and open the outside walls.

Another set of asymmetrical groin vaults exists in the cloister out-side the southern nave aisle at Tournus. To help absorb the pressure exerted by the nave vaults on the aisle walls, masons raised the height of the cloister vaults by pointing the webs adjacent to the nave walls

47. Tournus, Saint-Philibert, interior, nave, southern aisle, second bay, vault and outside wall (detail of Fig. 46); (*a*) semicircular *formeret;* (*b*) drooping groin web.

(Figs. 48, 49). These webs reach approximately the height of the crossing of the groins in the cloister. To channel this weight effectively, they lowered the height of vaults on the outside of the cloister by making the outside webs semicircular. The angle of descent was increased further by lowering the springing of the webs on the outside compared with the springing of the webs adjacent to the nave. Below the springing of these webs, massive half-cylindrical buttresses on the outside wall stabilize this steeply descending weight. The asymmetrical vaults

48. Tournus, Saint-Philibert, interior, cloister, with asymmetrical webs.

in the cloister were built with standard southern brick-based devices: a steeply corbeled base, a true vault with relatively horizontal and straight groin lines, and a flattened crown and pointed inside web.

In southern Burgundy, perhaps the most striking example of an asymmetrical vault can be found in the ambulatory of the priory church at Paray-le-Monial (Fig. 50). In this groin vault, the arrises cross much more toward the inside than the outside of the vault, and the web on the inside of the vault springs higher than the web on the outside of the vault.[8] Two objectives were accomplished by making the

49. Tournus, Saint-Philibert, interior, cloister, northern wall, with pointed web.

vault asymmetrical. Builders used the asymmetrical arrises to compensate for the irregular outline of the trapezoidal ambulatory bay. This adjustment allowed them to make the groin lines more or less straight, thereby saving themselves a lot of trouble in constructing scaffolding over this wide space. The high springing of the interior web and the low placement and pitch of the exterior web also could be used to channel the thrust from the half dome of the apse onto the low outside walls and radiating chapels of the ambulatory. Inside the ambulatory, a *tas-de-charge* reinforces the pressure points of the vault webs on these walls; the large ashlar on the bottom of the transverse arches courses with similar stones in the corbeled portions of the groins on the outside wall. On the inside wall, at the base of the vault, the oversized voussoirs in the springing of the transverse arches course with similar stones in the arcades.

50. Paray-le-Monial, priory church, interior, ambulatory, vaults.

The Pointed Transverse Arch

Burgundian masons not only changed the structure, construction, and aesthetics of the Italian brick vault but also added an important feature: They pointed the transverse arch beneath the pointed web. Instead of laying the web, and the filler stones beneath the web, directly on a round-headed arch, they now distinctly pointed the extrados of the arch.

In southern Europe at the beginning of the eleventh century, masons occasionally pointed the transverse arch. They sometimes pointed the diaphragm wall above the arch, as seen in the crypt of Sainte-Marie at Levens in the Alpes Maritimes (Fig. 51). Alternatively, they lengthened the archivolts in the center of the arch, in effect heightening the arch by expanding the circumference of the extrados at its peak. This technique is used with bricks in the crypt of Sant'Eusebio at Pavia, as well as with brick-shaped stones in the arcade of the nave of Saint-Martin at Chapaize. Although they occasionally extended the top of the extrados, they always left the intrados, on the bottom of the arch, as a rounded segment of a circle.

In Catalonia at the beginning of the eleventh century, masons extended central voussoirs more often and for more functions than ma-

51. Levens, Sainte-Marie, interior, crypt, detail of transverse arch and groin vault.

sons in any other region of the littoral. Two reasons explain their decision. First, the availability of quarried stone allowed them to shape
voussoirs in an endless variety of sizes. Lombard masons, in contrast,
could not easily vary the size of voussoirs because they usually built
with bricks or found stones, like riverbed rocks; these materials are
relatively small, and in the case of bricks, premolded or precut. Second,
masons in Catalonia could tap the Arabic tradition of horseshoe arches.
Such arches in important late tenth-century Catalan churches, like
those at Cuxa, Roda, and Ripoll, provided a model for masons who
extended the central voussoirs in brick-based churches.[9]

There are many examples of lengthened central arcade stones in
the eleventh-century, brick-based church of Saint-Martin-du-Canigou.
Long central voussoirs heighten the extrados of the central apse door

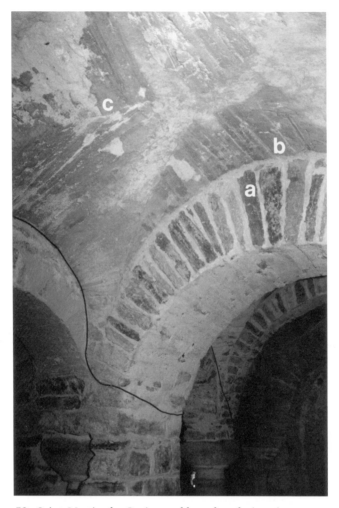

52. Saint-Martin-du-Canigou, abbey church, interior, crypt, detail of transverse arch and groin vault; (*a*) enlarged central voussoirs; (*b*) raised crown line; (*c*) diagonal arris.

and create a focal point over this important portal. In the transverse arches in the crypt, the extended length of the central voussoirs raises the height of the extrados under the groin vaults (Fig. 52a). This added height of the extrados raises the crown line of the webs that rest on the transverse arches. The increased web height, in turn, allows webs with a narrow circumference (Fig. 52b) to reach the same level as the long diagonal arrises (Fig. 52c).

In the side aisles of the nave of Sant Llorenç de Morunys, masons similarly heightened the webs in groin vaults by lengthening the cen-

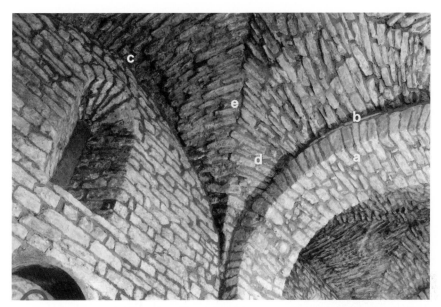

53. Sant Llorenç de Morunys, abbey church, interior, nave, northern aisle, first bay, detail of wall, groin vault, and transverse arch; (*a*) enlarged central voussoirs; (*b*) horizontal filler stones above the extrados of the transverse arch; (*c*) pointed outside wall; (*d*) in corbeled web, horizontally laid stones course through arris; (*e*) in true vault, on either side of the arris, stones neither touch each other nor consistently course with stones in the web.

tral stones in the arcade and transverse arches (Fig. 53a) and by in-serting horizontal filler stones above the extrados (Fig. 53b). In each bay, they also raised the outside groin web to the same height as the diagonal arrises by stacking the outside-wall stones into a point and resting the groin web on top of it (Fig 53c).

The late eleventh-century church of Sant Cugat de Salou provides a particularly sophisticated example of extended central voussoirs (Fig. 54). In the apse arcade of the north transept, as is common in brick-based Catalan architecture, the length of the central voussoirs increases while the intrados remains semicircular. In a startling development, however, masons changed the profile of each arcade stone to exagger-ate the difference between the heightened peak of the extrados and the rounded intrados. They emphasized the raised central extrados by increasingly undercutting the voussoirs toward the center of the arch (Fig. 54a), while narrowing the fascia of the same stones (Fig. 54b).

Pointing the extrados of arches made the task of building pointed webs much simpler. Masons no longer needed to build pointed walls above the arches in order to support pointed webs. Instead, they could avoid this tricky and labor-intensive step in construction by resting the centering and lag boards for pointed webs directly on a pointed voussoir frame. They could also dispense with the filler stones and diaphragm arches that throughout the southern littoral had been used to lay lag boards for pointed webs. The aisle vault at Farges combines the old and new technology, offering a glimpse into the process of change surrounding the pointed arch (see Fig. 45). In these vaults, a pointed row of filler stones still supports the pointed web, but a pointed extrados in the arch beneath this row of filler stones also raises the web to a new height.

In the aisle vaults at Farges, as elsewhere in Burgundy at the end of the eleventh century, masons began to point the intrados on the bottom, as well as the extrados on top, of the arch. This step did not markedly affect the construction or shape of the pointed webs. As we have seen, pointing the webs of groin vaults had occurred long before pointing the bottom, or even the top, of the arches beneath them. The change was important for aesthetic reasons, however, because by pointing the intrados of arches, masons could increase the amount of light and space passing between the low bays. At the level of the crown of the vault, the visitor could have an uninterrupted view down the aisles.

A structural advantage also is gained by pointing the intrados of arches. Compared with semicircular arches, pointed arches direct the weight from the vault more efficiently to isolated spots beneath them. This benefit is especially important in a church like the one at Farges, where masons used transverse barrels instead of groin vaults in the aisles. In a transverse barrel, the entire weight from the vault descends toward the sides of the vault, where the transverse arches that cross the aisle have to stabilize the pressure. In an effort to make transverse arches more structurally efficient, masons pointed the arches, and this improvement relieved some of the load from the vault on them. They further reduced the load on the crown of the arches by "breaking" the web. The continuous weight from the transverse barrel is isolated into small webs that descend into points at the edges of the vault. On the outside corner, they supported these points with buttresses, and on the inside corner, where the arcades and transverse arches meet, they braced them with converging large ashlar blocks.

54. Sant Cugat de Salou, interior, transept, northern apse, arcade; (*a*) undercut voussoirs in center of arch; (*b*) narrow fascia of central voussoirs.

The Corbel Table and Buttresses

Another structural benefit of pointing an arch is that it allows weight to descend at a more vertical angle than in round-headed construction. As it descends at a steep angle, the weight from the vault, transmitted through the pointed arch, hits the outside wall at a lower level than if it had passed through a semicircular arch. At Farges, for example, masons not only pointed the transverse arch but also increased its angle of springing. These changes allow the arch to spring below the middle of the window instead of higher up the aisle wall (see Fig. 45f).

As masons learned to direct most of the weight from the arch and vault below the midpoint of the aisle wall, they no longer needed to use the area under the eaves to absorb this pressure. They were free to change radically the structure and appearance of the upper part of the wall. In particular, corbel tables could be eliminated. Throughout southern Europe, in the first part of the century, masons had used the relieving arches in corbel tables – sunk like transverse barrel vaults inside the wall – to stabilize the walls that support vaults. In the brick churches in northern Italy, this system of corbel tables had been introduced primarily in the apse. In early eleventh-century Italian brick

55. Milan, Sant'Eustorgio, exterior, apse.

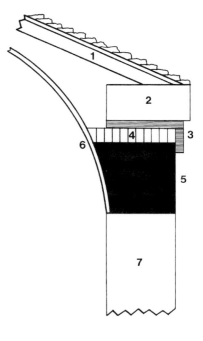

Drawing 4. Cross section of Milanese early eleventh-century apse: (1) roof beams, (2) wall with decorative string-courses, (3) corbel table with bricks laid length-wise (stretchers), (4) arches with radially laid bricks, (5) open niches, (6) half dome, (7) wall.

churches like Sant'Eustorgio in Milan (Fig. 55, Drawing 4), vault-ed niches and/or corbel tables – placed within the apse wall itself – strengthen the wall sufficiently to receive the weight from the apse dome. In contrast, except in northern Italian churches with very high walls, there is no need to use corbel tables to stabilize the central-vessel walls because they are almost always unvaulted.

56. Farges, Saint-Barthélemy, exterior, nave, southern aisle wall.

In the side aisle at Farges, masons were able to eliminate not only corbel tables but also the upper portion of the buttresses beneath the eaves (Fig. 56). Massive, projecting buttresses support the pressure from the vault on the lower portion of the aisle wall. On the sloping southern side of the nave, they reinforced the bottom of the buttresses with oversized ashlar, and widened the buttresses below the midpoint of the wall. The widening of the flat surface of the buttresses corresponds to the widening of the circumference of the respond on the interior of the southern aisle wall (visible on the right in Fig. 42).

CLUNY III

In southern Burgundy, ashlar routinely was used by the twelfth century. In the aisles of small buildings like the one at Farges, and in major buildings like the abbey churches at Cluny and Paray-le-Monial, masons coupled the pointed arch on the interior with buttresses on the exterior. This support system is interactive, in the sense that it links responds and pointed webs and arches on the interior with isolated buttresses on the bottom of the exterior wall. These interpenetrating parts that punctuate the fabric of the building encouraged masons to rethink the typical brick-based wall that had survived from the First Romanesque period. In that earlier type of wall, regular small stones

57. Chapaize, Saint-Martin, exterior, crossing tower; (*a*) relieving arch.

course horizontally without interruption, and corbel tables and thin projecting bands outline the surface as a horizontal, relieving-arch system (Fig. 57; see Fig. 3).

In the lower aisles of Cluny III, in the corner of each bay, massive ashlar responds (Fig. 58) and buttresses (Fig. 59) vertically interrupt the continuous courses of the wall, and classically based decoration surrounds these isolated ashlar parts. Masons peppered the inside of the building with capitals, columns, and pilasters, and lined the exterior with *cyma recta* brackets, cavetto-and-torus plinths, and string-course moldings.

58. Cluny III, interior, choir, southern aisle wall.

At Cluny III, brick techniques of local construction were integrated with these ashlar decoration and supports. Masons laid most of the interior and exterior aisle wall with homogeneous, brick-shaped stones;[10] coursed these stones in relatively small, regular beds – usually without extending framing stones next to the ashlar piers and buttresses; and surrounded jambs and window voussoirs with brick-shaped stones.

To build the pointed vaults at Cluny III, masons also followed the local brick tradition, as seen in the ruined cross section of the groin vault in the southern aisle of the choir. Brick-shaped stones are used

59. Cluny III, exterior, nave, southern aisle, bays six and seven, buttresses before reconstruction in 1996.

in the major section of the *formeret,* which supports the groin vault in the outside aisle (Fig. 60a). Horizontally coursed, brick-shaped stones, corbeled directly into the aisle wall, are used in the lower portion of the aisle groin (Fig. 60b).

The type of construction in the corbeled base changes in the true-vault portion of the groin. In the corbeled base of the vault, the stones of the arris course directly into the stones of the web (Figs. 61a, 62a), whereas in the true-vault section of the groin, the stones of the arris form a separate vertical spine (Figs. 61b, 62b). The stones in the spine largely do not course with the stones in the web (Figs. 61c, 62c), which presumably was set after the spine was laid.[11] A separate spine of stones above a corbeled base can also be observed in the ambulatory vaults in the Cluniac priory church at Paray-le-Monial (see Fig. 50).

This difference in the technique of laying corbeled and noncorbeled stones existed for a long time in brick-based construction. In the side-aisle vaults at Sant Llorenç de Morunys, for example, in the corbeled

60. Cluny III, interior, choir, southern aisle, ruined central transverse arch and *formerets* (detail of Fig. 58); (*a*) brick-shaped *formeret* stones; (*b*) horizontally coursed stones in corbeled portion of groin vault; (*c*) ashlar *tas-de-charge* at base of *formeret* and transverse arch; (*d*) horizontally coursed brick-shaped stones in center of springing of transverse arch.

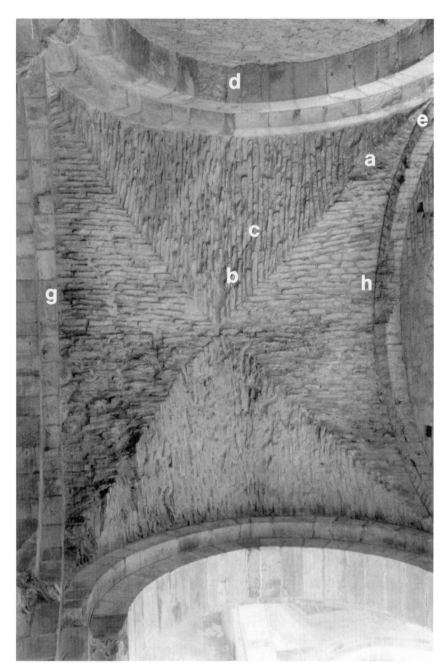

61. Cluny III, interior, nave, southern aisle, eastern bay; (*a*) stones in corbeled base of groin web course through arris; (*b*) spine of stones in arris do not course with (*c*) loosely laid stones of true vault; (*d*) pointed double order of voussoirs in transverse arch; (*e*) corbeled section of web rests above *tas-de-charge;* (*g*) high order beneath inside web; (*h*) single semicircular order of brick-shaped stones in *formeret.*

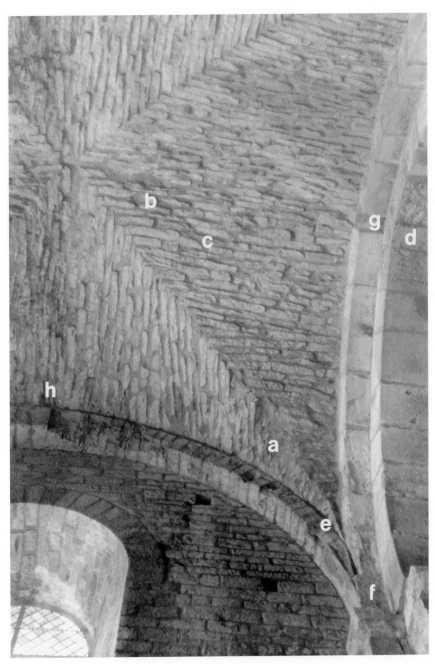

62. Cluny III, interior, nave, southern aisle, eastern bay; (*a*) stones in corbeled base of groin web course through arris; (*b*) spine of stones in arris do not course with (*c*) loosely laid stones of true vault; (*d*) pointed double order of voussoirs in transverse arch; (*e*) corbeled section of web rests above *tas-de-charge;* (*f*) *tas-de-charge* at springing of *formeret* and transverse arch; (*g*) high order beneath inside web; (*h*) single semicircular order of brick-shaped stones in *formeret.*

63. Cluny III, interior, nave, southern aisle, eastern bay, groin vault.

base, the stones cross the arris line (see Fig. 53d) and course with the stones in the webs. In contrast, in the true-vault portion of the groin, on either side of the arris, the stones form a spine; they do not touch each other (see Fig. 53e) or consistently course with the stones in the webs. Similarly in the true-vault portion of the aisle vault at Chapaize (see Fig. 36), masons carefully laid the stones along the groin lines in an alternating and overlapping spine pattern that does not align consistently with the courses in the adjacent webs.

At Cluny III and at Paray-le-Monial, masons took similar steps to those taken at Farges to improve the structure and construction of groin vaults. They used the brick technique of pointing the short lat-

64. Paray-le-Monial, interior, nave, southern aisle, eastern bay, groin vault.

eral webs, but they improved this structure by pointing the transverse arches beneath the groin webs (Figs. 61d, 62d), eliminating the lowest section of corbeled web masonry (Figs. 61e, 62e), and extending the pointed profile of the web from the outside of the vault almost to the crossing (Figs. 63, 64). They also incorporated the southern brick techniques of keeping the groins relatively straight and flattening them at the crown, but improved the vault's efficiency by increasing its angle of descent.

At Cluny, masons also modified the brick technique of coursing the corbel vaults into the wall. Following the pattern observed in the aisles

at Chapaize (see Fig. 37), they created a wide and stable structural platform by coursing the brick-shaped stones in the corbel vault and aisle
wall with the brick-shaped stones inside the center of the transverse
arch (see Fig. 60d). They improved the brick system by replacing the
lowest portion of the vaults – the part that looks like a continuous order in southern First Romanesque construction (see Fig. 53) – with an
armature of ashlar (see Fig. 62f). At Lomello, a similar device exists,
in which single bricks laid at the base of the vault support both the
formeret and web (see Fig. 19). On the aisle wall of the nave and choir,
the masons at Cluny updated this technique by securing with a single
ashlar block the base of the brick-shaped *formerets* and groin vaults (see
Fig. 60c). At the springing of each *formeret,* a *tas-de-charge* combines in
one colossal stone the lower portions of the *formeret* and the first order
of the transverse arch.

Masons also strengthened the ashlar arches above the freestanding
piers. Doubling the orders of the arcade (see Fig. 61g) and transverse
arches (see Fig. 62g) increases the width and height of the frame below the vault. The increased width of the arch frame allows the span
of the vault to be narrower. The increased height of the arcade and
transverse arches above the freestanding piers allows the webs on the
inside of the aisles to be higher (see Fig. 61g) than the webs on the
outside of the aisles (see Figs. 61h, 62h). The *formerets* supporting the
webs on the outside of the aisles are not doubled but instead are made
of one small order of brick-shaped stones.

In the aisles of Cluny III, asymmetrical webs produce the same
structural advantages as the asymmetrical webs in the aisles at Tournus
and Farges. The outside webs can be made longer and lower, and
therefore more vertical, than the inside webs. This increased vertical
angle allows the outside webs to channel the weight from the vault
to the ground more efficiently than in webs with a more diagonal
angle.[12]

By the time of Cluny III, masons had also learned to minimize the
webs of the vault. In the freestanding arches of the aisles, they combined a regular ashlar frame and a pointed arch to support the smallest and lightest possible webs. The introduction of a solid frame of double ashlar orders and a massive *tas-de-charge* allowed them to reduce
the brick-shaped stones in the true-vault portion of the groin to relatively small, flat webs.

Strengthening the framing system also permitted the process of building pointed vaults to be reduced. Once masons learned to point the top of the arch, they could eliminate the built-up layer of filler stones that in brick-based construction had been needed to lay the centering and lag boards for pointed webs. As they came to rely on ashlar pointed arches to frame these webs, they could also eliminate or reduce the corbel vault as a construction platform to build the true vault.

In the aisles of Cluny III, the ashlar arch frame is a different shape and material from the brick-based vault and wall, and these differences in appearance and construction may have encouraged masons to reconsider the visual relationship among the structural parts. I am not implying that, because we speak separately of construction, structure, and aesthetics in this building, masons categorized them in this way, approached them as separate "problems," or solved them sequentially – one before another. The fact is, however, that as masons increasingly introduced ashlar arches and supports, they had to modify the long-standing tradition of formulating decisions based on the shape of brick. Previously, local masons trained in brick construction had easily merged the corbel vault, with its base leg, into the vertically continuous, square-edged reveals of the walls and supports. While the masons at Cluny also made the walls and vaults of brick-shaped stones, they now had to master the horizontal interruptions inherent in an ashlar frame system. They were challenged to integrate the vertically continuous aesthetic of brick construction with ashlar arches that sever groin vaults at their base. To articulate the interruption in shapes and material at the juncture of the vault, wall, and support, they introduced classically based impost moldings, capitals, and colonnettes.

CONCLUSION

The vaults in the aisles of Cluny III represent not so much a revolutionary breakthrough, or the culmination of a local tradition, as a unique work in progress. More humans than heroes, the masons at Cluny did not invent or import wholesale a new method of building vaults and arches. Rather, they improved the system of brick-based, pointed-web construction that local masons had used in groin vaults for almost a century. They refined the efficiency and strength of the framework of the vault, minimized the corbeled and true-vault webs, and merged brick and ashlar masonry traditions to improve construction and structure. They used these practical improvements to create thin and penetrated walls, high and wide spaces, and an articulation based on sculptural carving and classically based architectural details.

CHAPTER

5

The Barrel Vault

 The barrel vault often is described as an interim solu-
tion that was superseded as soon as masons under-
stood the advantages of point support for large-scale
groin and rib vaults. I briefly shall show the other side
of the story and demonstrate that, at the beginning
of the eleventh century, masons often used the same
system of construction and structure to build both
groin and barrel vaults. This overlap in the technique
of building these two vaults supports the view that masons did not
conceive the barrel as a lesser vault form or treat it apart from the isolated, arched framework of groin vaults.

TOURNUS UPPER NARTHEX

The longitudinal barrel vault in the upper narthex at Tournus provides
an ideal opportunity to study the construction of the barrel vault, because the stones in these three bays are almost completely exposed
(Fig. 65).[1] Three distinct steps were used to build the barrel in the central vessel and the two half barrels in the aisles.

1. Masons first constructed transverse arches. It is understandable that
    they would have used narrow arches to build vaults because,
    compared with vaults, arches require less labor and a smaller
    wooden centering to erect. These arches provide an armature to
    support the minimal centering and lag boards for the true vault.

65. Tournus, Saint-Philibert, interior, upper narthex, facing east.

2. The masons then built the lower segment of the barrel as a corbel vault. In this construction, the stones horizontally course into the outside wall, and these courses progressively cantilever away from the vertical plane of the wall. The corbel vault provides a firm base to receive the pressure from the radially laid stones of the true vault.[2]

3. With the transverse arch and corbel vault in place, the masons erected a centering with lag boards. These wooden forms were used to lay a true vault above the corbeled base.

66. Tournus, Saint-Philibert, interior, upper narthex, central barrel vault, northern face, first transverse arch; (*a*) horizontally coursed stones in corbeled portion of vault; (*b*) corbeled portion of vault overlaps side of transverse arch; (*c*) square stone covering putlog hole; (*d*) unevenly coursed stones in true vault; (*e*) stones in true vault continue above extrados of transverse arch; (*f*) cantilevered stringcourse molding.

In the central vessel of the upper narthex at Tournus (Fig. 66), masons first erected transverse arches, and with this armature in place, laid the fifteen lowest courses on either side of the vault (Fig. 66a).[3] This sequence can be determined by observing the position of the horizontally coursed stones in the vault in relation to the radially laid stones in the transverse arches. The lower courses of the vault are laid in corbeled beds that collide with the sides of each transverse arch (Figs. 66b, 67) rather than continue above the stones of the arch. In the last courses of the corbel vault, masons left putlog holes to insert the beams for the centering of the true vault; these holes later were filled with square stones (Fig. 66c).

After the transverse arches and corbel vault were built, masons erected wooden centering with lag boards to lay the stones for the true vault. A number of changes in masonry indicate such a structure was used. At the level of the true vault, above approximately the fifteenth bed, the coursing abruptly switches from regular rows of horizontally laid stones to irregular beds that form a swirling pattern (Fig. 66d). This loose arrangement of stones could not have been possible without the support of centering and lag boards during construction. Masons probably braced the beams on the transverse arches, laid the vault stones on lag boards, and continued this masonry over and above each arch (Fig. 66e). The stones in the true vault are different from the stones in the corbel vault, because they continue above the extrados of the arch stones instead of running into the sides of the voussoirs.

Corbeling the lower part of the vault saves materiel and labor and increases structural efficiency. Up to approximately 25 percent of the height of the vault, masons needed neither the wooden centering that is required to build a real vault, nor transverse arches that may have been used to brace the centering. They simply extended the horizontal courses from the wall into a corbel vault.

Most of the stress from a vault usually comes at about 25 percent of the height of the web; therefore, by making the base a massive, coursed extension of the wall, masons were able to stabilize the weight from the true vault at a critical level. In the central vessel at Tournus, the corbeled portion of the vault also is cantilevered on a projecting stringcourse molding (Fig. 66f).[4] This continuous ledge is built of stones longer and wider than those used in the wall below it (Figs. 65, 68). The extra projection on the inside of the nave enables the weight from the vault to descend more to the center than to the outside of the wall. This slight adjustment to the location of the pressure on the wall allows for thinner walls with more openings.

The same techniques that were used to build the barrel vault in the nave were used to build the half-barrel vaults in the aisles (Fig. 68).[5]

67. Tournus, Saint-Philibert, interior, upper narthex, first bay, northern wall, detail of transverse arch and barrel vault; corbel vault overlaps side of transverse arch.

Masons first built transverse arches and then extended the wall adjacent to them as a corbel vault, approximately 25 percent of the height of the half barrel (Fig. 69a). As in the central vessel, evidence of this sequence of construction can be found in the relation of the stones in the vault to the stones in the arches and vault. The masonry in the corbeled portion of the vault abuts the sides of the voussoirs in the transverse arches (Fig. 69b), and the lower courses of the transverse arch extend as a spur buttress into the fabric of the wall behind the corbeled stones. The corbel vault and spur buttresses provide a solid base – coursed into the exterior wall – to support the true vault and transverse arches.

As in the barrel in the central vessel, in the half barrel in the aisles, at about a quarter of the height of the vault, the construction of the

68. Tournus, Saint-Philibert, interior, upper narthex, southern side aisle.

web changes from a corbel to a true vault. This shift can be deduced from changes in the web masonry. At this level, the stones change from overlapping the sides of each transverse arch to resting on the extrados above it (Fig. 69c). At approximately the same height, the transverse arch also changes from a spur buttress, with horizontally laid stones (Fig. 69b), to a true arch, whose voussoirs radiate from a center (Fig. 69c).

Wooden centering was needed to support the true-vault sections of the barrel vaults in the central and side aisles. As in the case of groin-

69. Tournus, Saint-Philibert, interior, upper narthex, northern side aisle, second transverse arch and adjacent half-barrel vault; (*a*) corbeled portion of vault overlaps (*b*) side of coursed base of transverse arch; (*c*) true-vault portion of the barrel continues above extrados of radially laid stones in transverse arch.

vault construction, in order to make this centering as light as possible, masons probably relied upon the stone voussoirs of the transverse arches to support the timber framework. This centering may have been flexible, so that as it bent under the weight of the lag boards and web stones, it secured a hold against the side of the transverse arches.[6] The vaults in the aisles of the early eleventh-century Roussillon church at

70. Elne, Sainte-Eulalie, interior, nave, northern side aisle, quarter-barrel vault, scaffold-beam holes in diaphragm arches.

Elne show a variant on this method, in which small, flexible beams of various sizes and shapes were used to lay barrel vaults. Traces of these small beams exist in the sides of the diaphragm arches (Fig. 70). The position of these holes in relation to the underside of the vault reveals that masons left just enough space between the beams and the vault stones to place lag boards.

In the upper narthex at Tournus, lag boards left an impression on the mortar in the easternmost bay of the central vessel (Fig. 71). These impressions show two features often found in the lag-board construction of barrel vaults. First, the top surface of the boards is aligned with the extrados of the transverse arches. This arrangement allows the bed of stones that rests on the lag boards to continue over and above the voussoirs in the transverse arches. Second, the outside edges of the small wooden lag boards also are vertically aligned. Masons carefully fitted the centering and lag boards in the space beneath the vault and between the sides of the transverse arches so that, once the mortar dried, they could easily knock down the woodwork – and probably reuse it – without disturbing the masonry in the vaults and transverse arches. The transverse arches, then, could have served in the constructional phase as a platform for wooden centering, and once the center-

71. Tournus, Saint-Philibert, interior, upper narthex, central vessel, third bay, barrel vault, impressions left by lag boards in mortar (author's detail photograph from restoration file, Caisse Nationale des Monuments Historiques).

ing was removed, as a structural brace for the walls beneath the vault. At the time of construction, the transverse arches may not have been necessary to support a cohesive web, but eventually they could have served a structural function. The masons likely may not have made this distinction, but if they had, looking to the future, they could have thought of this framework of stone arches as a precautionary structure in case instability or infiltration in the mortar caused the stones in the vault webs to lose adhesion.[7]

From this description at Tournus, I do not want to leave the impression that masons relied solely on transverse arches to build barrel

72. Uchizy, Saint-Pierre, interior, nave, central vessel, facing west.

vaults. Experience has shown me that, in southern Burgundy during the Romanesque period, masons used multiple techniques, often in combination, to lay the true-vault portion of barrel vaults. In the nave of the neighboring church at Uchizy, for example, masons erected transverse arches and pronounced imposts, and below either side of the imposts they projected small rectangular blocks (Fig. 72). These devices probably were used to support the ends of horizontal beams that spanned the central vessel and carried some of the centering for the true vault. In the southern side aisle of the church at Brancion, at

73. Brancion, Saint-Pierre, interior, nave, northern side aisle, half-barrel vault; (*a*) corbel block to support scaffolding; (*b*) impressions in mortar left by lag boards.

the level that the half barrel springs from the outside wall, similar rectangular blocks project on the inside wall (Fig. 73a). Again, these blocks were probably used to support the horizontal beams that carried the centering for lag boards across the aisle. As in the vault at Tournus, traces left in the mortar show that masons arranged the outside edges of these lag boards so that they would align vertically (Fig. 73b).

To make and insert these projecting rectangular blocks would have been easy. All the masons had to do was to project an extra-long stone from a bed in the wall. What makes the examples at Uchizy and Brancion exceptional is that once the masons removed the centering, they did not trim the part of the stones that projected. Had they done so, we may not have been able to distinguish these particular blocks from other stones that course normally in the wall.

To build the barrel vaults at Tournus, then, masons followed the same techniques masons had used throughout southern Europe to build groin vaults with pointed webs. In both barrel and groin vaults, they first built a framework of round-headed transverse arches to divide the vault into a series of cells. They then secured the base of the vault with corbeled construction. Finally, they could have used these arches to brace the centering that supported lag boards for the true vault. In both vault types, the same system of isolated arch supports is used to build and support the webs.

Given these similarities in construction and structure between the barrel and groin vaults, it seems unlikely that First Romanesque masons thought of the groin vault as fundamentally different from, or better than, the barrel vault. There is also little evidence to support the conclusion that, having recognized the superiority of the groin vault, masons abandoned the barrel vault and systematically replaced it with the groin. Instead, the evidence shows that masons in Burgundy worked for generations to combine the two vault types.

Masons considered these vaults similar formal, constructive, and structural devices, and used the special properties of each to improve the other. The fact that a barrel creates continuous thrust and a groin points of pressure did not change masons' approach to the basic issues of vaulting. For each type of vault, they insisted on the same vocabulary of brick-shaped stones and sought the same benefits of labor and materiel by minimizing the true-vault span. They also achieved these goals with a corbel-vault base and an isolated framework of round-headed arches.

VAULTING PARALLELS IN CATALONIA AND BURGUNDY

In Catalonia, as in Burgundy, in the first half of the eleventh century, corbels and true vaults were combined in barrel-vault construction. In Sant Pere at Ager, in the apse of the northern transept masons used different types of masonry to construct these two sections of the vault. Regularly coursed, brick-shaped stones in the corbel vault (Fig. 74a) extend without interruption into the vertical plane of the apse wall. At the level of the true vault (about a quarter the height of the half dome), after a distinct horizontal suture, stones of a more irregular size, shape, and coursing replace these evenly coursed, brick-shaped stones (Fig. 74b). It would have been necessary to use lag boards to build the irregular and radiating stones of the overhanging true vault, but not the regular horizontal masonry beneath it.

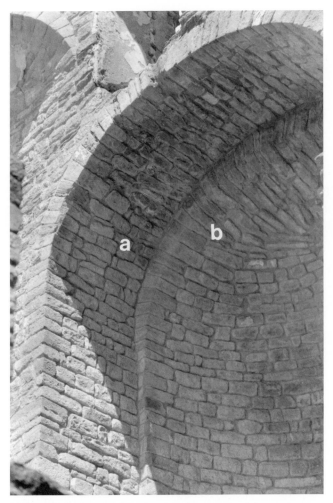

74. Ager, Sant Pere, interior, northern apse; (*a*) evenly coursed, brick-shaped stones in corbeled portion of half dome; (*b*) true-vault portion of half dome.

In the central vessel of the abbey church of Sant Vicenç at Cardona, masons again used transverse arches, corbeled webs, and true vaults to build the barrel vault. As in the upper narthex at Tournus, two distinct stages of vault construction are visible to either side of the transverse arch in the western bay.[8] The even courses of brick-shaped stones in the clerestory extend into the corbeled bottom quarter of the vault (see Fig. 11a), where they abut the sides of the transverse arch (see Fig. 11b). After a distinct horizontal suture, irregularly sized and loosely

75. Saint-Michel-de-Cuxa, interior, crypt, lateral nave, central vessel, first transverse arch and adjacent barrel vault; (*a*) corbel vault, impressions left by lag boards overlap side of transverse arch; (*b*) true vault, impressions left by lag boards continue above extrados of transverse arch.

coursed stones begin to make up the true vault (see Fig. 11c). These stone courses extend above the extrados of the arch, without abutting the sides of the arch (see Fig. 11d). To rest beams for the centering of the true vault, in the last courses of the corbel vault masons left putlog holes, which they later filled with square stones (see Fig. 11e).

Impressions of lag boards no longer survive in the vault at Cardona, but they can still be seen throughout the vaults in the crypt of the

76. Paray-le-Monial, priory church, interior, choir, barrel vault, northern face. (*a*) regular beds of rectangular stones in corbeled portion of vault; (*b*) irregular masonry in true vault.

nearby abbey church of Saint-Michel-de-Cuxa. These impressions reveal the shift from corbel- to true-vault construction. In the first bay of the central vessel, as they finished the corbel vault, masons began to use lag boards in preparation for laying the stones of the true vault. The impressions show that they abutted the corbeled stones, as well as the lag boards in front of them, into the side of the arches (Fig. 75a). When they reached the level of the true vault, however, the masons needed to use the support of transverse arches to lay the vault stones, and therefore at this level, they continued the stones and the lag boards that supported them, above the extrados of the arches (Fig. 75b).

To summarize, in the first half of the eleventh century, in both Burgundy and Catalonia, to build barrel vaults masons frequently erected a transverse arch, abutted the lower part of the arch with stones from a corbel vault, and used the upper voussoirs of the arch to support the centering and lag boards for the true vault. In Burgundy in the twelfth century, this system continued to be used, even for pointed barrel vaults. In the choir of the abbey church at Paray-le-Monial, masons corbeled the lower quarter of the barrel vault with regular beds of rectangular stones (Fig. 76a). This stonework resembles the masonry in the wall below it, but it contrasts with the irregularly shaped and un-evenly laid masonry in the true vault above it (Fig. 76b).[9]

In the central vessel of Saint-Pierre at Brancion, masons used dis-tinctly visible steps to erect the central barrel vault. An arcade (with the vaulted aisle behind it) stabilizes and supports the weight from the vault and transverse arches. Above the arcade, a setback (Fig. 77a) with putlog holes (Fig. 77b) and corbels provides a place to rest the beams and planks for the next stage of building. Above the arcade, enormous imposts also support the centering for the transverse arches.

Once the transverse arch was built, masons erected the corbel vault that now overlaps it. In the corbeled lower quarter of the barrel vault (Fig. 77c), even beds of rectangular stones, like those in the spandrels of the nave wall, abut the sides of the transverse arches (Fig. 77d). At the level of the true vault, however, they would have needed center-ing and lag boards to lay the stones. At this level, they would have used the arch itself to help support the centering for the vault. The masonry here changes to more loosely laid radiating stones that continue above the extrados of the transverse arches, without abutting the sides of the arches (Fig. 77e).

77. Brancion, Saint-Pierre, interior, nave, second bay, southern wall, detail of arcade and barrel vault; (*a*) setback; (*b*) putlog hole; (*c*) corbeled portion of vault, with even beds of rectangular stones that (*d*) overlap the side of transverse arch; (*e*) true vault, with impressions of lag boards, whose loosely laid stones continue above extrados of transverse arch.

CHAPTER

6

Systems of Arch Support

Formerets and transverse arches, the framework of arches around the pointed vault, so far have been considered in the context of construction and articulation. I now shall analyze these arches in a broad structural context, to show how attached and free-standing arches brace the vault cell and stabilize the walls surrounding the vault.

In brick-based churches at the turn of the eleventh century, masons frequently used *formerets* and transverse arches as relieving arches. These arches have a similar function to that of corbel tables under eaves, wall arcades in apses, and voussoirs and cover stones surrounding portals and windows. In other words, builders did not treat the arches beneath groin vaults as a separate type of armature specifically designed to support groin webs, but rather as one of a network of relieving arches throughout the church. In the apse and choir at Sant Vicenç at Cardona, for example, cover stones relieve the pressure, from the roof, vault, and upper wall, on the voussoirs that link the spur buttresses (Fig. 78).[1] Arches also stabilize the aisle walls: On the exterior they function as a continuous corbel table that reinforces the wall at the level that the groin vaults impact it; and on the inside they act as *formerets* (Fig. 79a) and transverse arches (Fig. 79b) that surround and brace the groin-vault webs.

113

78. Cardona, Sant Vicenç, exterior, intersection of apse and northern choir wall; spur buttresses, voussoirs, and relieving cover stones.

WALL AND BUTTRESSES IN NORTHERN EUROPE

At the beginning of the eleventh century, in major cathedrals in northern France like those at Auxerre, Chartres, Clermont-Ferrand, and Orléans, a different system was used to stabilize vault pressure, particularly in the central apse. Instead of placing relieving arches high inside the apse wall to stabilize the pressure from the half dome, masons channeled the thrust from the apse outside to the ambulatory and radiating chapels. In the chevet at Vignory (see Fig. 9), a descending series of vaults in the ambulatory and radiating chapels reinforces the wall beneath the half dome of the central apse. Ashlar and isolated vertical supports brace the walls in the chapels and ambulatory, where the weight moving down these vaults is grounded. In particular, ashlar jambs, quoins, and buttresses strengthen the structural weak spots at corners, around openings, and between walls.

A good example of the northern French approach to reinforcing the wall beneath a vault can be seen in the two-story transept chapels at Saint-Rémi at Reims (see Fig. 7). Instead of using continuously coursed brick-sized stones to brace the wall from the pressure of the piggybacked half domes, masons girdled the vault pressure with massive, isolated, and closely spaced ashlar buttresses. The two-story apse is essentially a passive structural skeleton surrounding a thick frame-and-fill wall. In typical northern fashion, horizontally tailored decoration

79. Cardona, Sant Vicenç, interior, nave, southern aisle; (*a*) *formerets;* (*b*) transverse arches.

interrupts these vertical ashlar members. At the top of the apse, the builders ignored southernisms like corbeled relieving arches and vertically continuous, square-edged brick-based reveals. Instead, they finished the apse with a cavetto stringcourse molding and capped each round buttress, as if it were a colonnette, with a capitallike impost.

In Ottonian churches, masons combined the benefits of southern brick-based and northern ashlar systems to stabilize vaults and walls. The standard buttressing technique found inside the apse wall of large, early eleventh-century, brick-based churches, like Sant'Eustorgio at Milan (see Fig. 55, Drawing 4) and Sant Vicenç at Cardona (see Fig. 78) is used to brace the half dome in the apse of the abbey church at Hersfeld (Fig. 80). Inside the wall, spur buttresses surround the springing of the vault, and connecting arches and small vaults strengthen these supports (Fig. 80a). An active system of small and large relieving arches, protected by rows of cover stones (Fig. 80b), stabilizes the groin vaults in the crypt (see Fig. 26).

At Hersfeld, isolated ashlar supports, typical of northern construction, also strengthen the wall surrounding the apse. Large ashlar but-

80. Hersfeld, abbey church, exterior, apse: (*a*) spur buttresses connected by arches and small vaults; (*b*) relieving arches with cover stones.

tresses and quoining, often found in German Roman and Carolingian buildings, brace both the exterior perimeter of the apse and the joint between the apse and choir walls. In the northern manner, a continuous stringcourse molding horizontally divides the apse and projecting imposts articulate the apse buttresses.[2]

Ottonian masons also used a combination of southern brick and northern ashlar techniques to strengthen walls that do not support vaults. In the abbey church at Limburg an der Haardt, for example, a typical southern arrangement of continuously coursed, brick-shaped masonry and a relieving system of corbel tables and Lombard bands stabilizes the high, unvaulted transept walls (Fig. 81). To support the crossing at the base of these walls, they also inserted large ashlar compound piers and articulated them with strong horizontal moldings.

Southern and northern building systems are combined again inside the walls of the north transept. A relieving arcade made from continuously coursed brick-based masonry and brick-shaped voussoirs brace the low walls (Fig. 82a). In this location, however, continuous southern articulation is not emphasized. The builders chose instead to support the arcade with closely spaced, classically based pilasters and to tailor these supports with strong horizontal imposts. This kind of wall arcade attached to horizontally interrupted pilasters appears as a stan-

81. Limburg an der Haardt, abbey church, nave, crossing and transept, with ashlar piers and Lombard corbel tables.

dard Ottonian structural device across northern Europe, from the exterior of the priory church at Hastière-par-Delà in Belgium to the interior of the crypt of the cathedral at Speyer. What makes the blend of northern and southern construction special at Limburg is the ease with which masons switched back and forth between the systems and incorporated the benefits of each one. In the north transept, as they turned from building the north wall to opening a wide arch into the nave aisle, they recognized that the relatively low and tightly spaced arcade pilasters no longer could be used to brace the wall. Their simple solution was to insert a southern system of corbel tables to relieve the pressure on the large aisle opening above the level of the pilaster imposts (Fig. 82b).

SOUTHERN RELIEVING ARCHES

Masons who built throughout the southern littoral rarely used the northern French system of exterior vaults in the form of an ambulatory with radiating chapels to relieve the pressure from the apse half dome. On the exterior of brick-based architecture throughout Catalonia, masons often used wall arches with niches and a corbel table of

82. Limburg an der Haardt, abbey church, interior, north transept; (*a*) pilaster arcade; (*b*) corbel table.

relieving arches to stabilize the wall at the level of the springing of the vault. Frequently, on the inside, below the vault, they further braced the wall by sinking a wall arcade into the fabric of the apse. This double system of internal supports, using an exterior corbel table and an interior wall arcade, exists in churches at Ager, Cardona, Gallifa, Granollers, Rosas, Sant Martí Sescorts, and many other Catalan locations. Wall arches on two levels laterally brace the apse and, when combined as at Ager (Fig. 83) and Cardona with small half domes above niches, also strengthen the wall from the diagonal pressure of the vault.

In Burgundy at the turn of the eleventh century, masons employed a similar system of relieving arches to reinforce the walls of brick-based buildings. They used corbel tables to stabilize high walls and all kinds of vault; and they used wall arcades below the half dome in the apse, projecting arches below the dome in the tower, and a framework of *formerets* and transverse arches beneath the groin vault in the aisles. In the apse, choir, and transept of Saint-Hippolyte at Combertault, masons lined the interior with relieving arches (Fig. 84) that penetrate the wall and stabilize it (Fig. 85). To strengthen the large expanse of wall surface on the high westwork of Saint-Vorles at Châtillon-sur-Seine, masons inserted corbel tables on the outside and semicircular

83. Ager, Sant Pere, interior, central apse, half dome and wall niches.

84. Combertault, Saint-Hippolyte, interior, choir and apse.

85. Combertault, Saint-Hippolyte, interior, intersection of choir and nave, northeast corner, detail of wall arcade.

wall arcades on the inside (Fig. 86). They also articulated these arcades in a manner typical of brick-based architecture in the region. At Combertault a necking of a double row of brick-shaped stones connects the wall arcade with a half-round pier, and at Châtillon the wall arcade becomes a continuous order that mimics the brick-shaped reveal of the arch.

A sophisticated arcaded relieving system frequently is used beneath the domed crossing of early brick-based buildings in southern Burgundy. The crossing is a structurally crucial location because that is where the transepts join the chevet and nave, and the weight of the vaulted tower impacts the building. Masons often used three or even four tiers of relieving arches in this location. In the tower of Saint-Martin at Chapaize, on the exterior at the level of the crossing dome, a corbel table relieves the thrust from the vault (Fig. 87). On successive levels of the interior, first wall arcades and transverse arches run between imposts (Fig. 88a), then squinches connected to corbel-table arches circle the

86. Châtillon-sur-Seine, Saint-Vorles, interior, westwork, upper story, wall arch.

87. Chapaize, Saint-Martin, exterior, southern wall below crossing tower, corbel table.

88. Chapaize, Saint-Martin, interior, crossing; (*a*) wall arcade, transverse arch; (*b*) squinch and corbel table; (*c*) vault window.

89. Bray, village church, interior, crossing; (*a*) wall arcade; (*b*) squinches and corbel table.

90. Laizé, Saint-Sulpice, interior, apse.

base of the dome (Fig. 88b), and finally voussoirs in the vault windows buttress the walls (Fig. 88c). These arches work on many levels to stabilize the wall surrounding the dome, and they perform a similar function as the relieving arches (see Fig. 57a) that reinforce the exterior wall above the openings on the second story of the tower. Inside the tower at Bray, masons used essentially the same system to project a wall arcade (Fig. 89a) and above it a continuous series of corbel tables and squinches (Fig. 89b).

A minuscule but strikingly beautiful version of this type of structure exists in the narrow apse tower of Saint-Sulpice at Laizé (Fig. 90). Masons reinforced the juncture of the dome and tower walls with corner squinches, and below this level braced the walls with corbeled arcades. They set these horizontally projecting semicircular arcades against rounded vertical apse walls and continued the soffits of the arcades directly into window arches. The result is a complex composition of dome, squinches, arcades, walls, and window arches that reads like a series of separate but intersecting small curved shapes. Inside the crossings at Chapaize, Bray, and Laizé, corbeled arches on multiple levels not only strengthen the walls beneath the vault but also reduce the span of the dome and direct the thrust of the vault more efficiently toward the center of the outside walls.[3]

91. Chapaize, Saint-Martin, exterior, nave, northern aisle, western bay.

Arcades, *formerets,* and transverse arches also are used to stabilize walls and relieve the pressure from groin vaults in the aisles. In the western bay of the northern aisle at Chapaize, on the exterior at the level of the springing of the groin vaults masons used corbel tables to strengthen the aisle wall (Fig. 91). On the interior, they stabilized the points on the wall where the groin webs descend by surrounding them with a perpendicular cage of arcades. An arcade supports the nave wall, a transverse arch connects the nave and outside aisle wall (some of the original brick-based voussoirs of the transverse arches can be seen on the right in Fig. 92), and *formerets* line the north and west faces of the aisle (see Fig. 37). Masons used these arches for many functions – to attach centering, lay lag boards, articulate the impost and upper edges of the vault, and absorb the specific pressure from the webs. The primary function of these arches, however, is to secure the walls from

92. Chapaize, Saint-Martin, interior, nave, northern aisle, second bay.

the pressure of the vaults. As in the aisle of Saint-Martin-de-Laives (Fig. 93), at each location where the groin webs descend, two *formerets* and a transverse arch meet to hold the springing of the vault in place. These radiating stones in the corbel tables, arcades, *formerets,* and transverse arches form an active, connected armature that reduces warping and contributes to the stability of the walls.

Mazille, Malay, and Cluny III

In brick-based buildings in southern Burgundy throughout the eleventh century, arches of all kinds continue to be used to brace the wall

93. Saint-Martin-de-Laives, interior, nave, southern aisle, detail of *formeret,* transverse arch, and groin vault.

from pressure exerted by the vault. A few miles south of Cluny, at Saint-Blaise at Mazille, to relieve the pressure of the vault dome on the apse wall, masons ran a corbel table beneath the eaves (Fig. 94) and stacked three concentric wall arcades above the windows (Fig. 95).[4] A *formeret* and two orders from the western face of the transverse arch converge to stabilize the springing of the pointed groin webs in the corners of the crossing (Fig. 96). These arches create an active ring of support around the base of the groin webs, and beneath the vault they articulate the crossing with analogous, continuous, square-edged, brick-based reveals.

At Notre-Dame at Malay, masons also used a combination of analogous wall arches to support the pressure from vaults.[5] In the apse, a corbel table (seen on the far right in Fig. 97) stabilizes the wall beneath

94. Mazille, Saint-Blaise, exterior, apse and choir, northern wall.

95. Mazille, Saint-Blaise, interior, apse, arcade.

96. Mazille, Saint-Blaise, interior, choir beneath tower, southern wall.

97. Malay, Notre-Dame, exterior, intersection of apse and choir, southern wall.

the half dome, and an extra arched reveal (Fig. 98a) strengthens the inside edge of the vault. Where these arches converge at the corner of the choir, a wall arch braces the wall beneath the barrel vault (Fig. 98b). In the crossing, a squinch and an extra order on either side of the transverse arches reinforce the walls beneath the dome (Fig. 98c).

In the chevet of both these churches, masons used the traditional brick-based technique of continuous coursing with almost no ashlar framing (see Figs. 94, 97). Working at the end of the eleventh century, they knew how to integrate buttresses, like those at the junction of the choir and apse, with the brick-based system of horizontal arches and corbel tables. In this location, where the exterior corbel table and the extra orders inside the apse and choir converge (Figs. 96, 98), they used isolated, vertical supports to stabilize the springing of the arches.

At Cluny III, arches in conjunction with buttresses also are used to brace walls from the pressure of vaults. In both the nave and choir, in each bay of the lower aisle masons placed a buttress on the outside (see Fig. 59) and a respond on the inside (see Fig. 58) at the position where the exterior wall arches (Fig. 99) and interior *formerets* and transverse arches come together (see Figs. 61, 62). As in traditional brick-based construction, the convergence of interior and exterior wall arches stabilizes the points where groin webs descend on the aisle wall. The combination of *formerets,* transverse arches, and exterior arcades also braces the bundles of responds and buttresses as pressure from the central barrel vault descends from the upper story through the transverse wall above each aisle vault onto the outside wall (Fig. 100).

This system of arches that girdle groin vaults goes back to experiments with corbel tables and wall arcades in the aisles of major regional brick-based buildings like those at Chapaize, Combertault, and Tournus. In the upper stories of the transept of Cluny III, masons again used this system of supporting arches but on a much larger scale. For generations, in buildings like the transept at Châtillon and the upper narthex at Tournus (Fig. 101), Burgundian masons had inserted corbel-table arches in the central vessel to stabilize the pressure from longitudinal barrels. Masons seem to have abandoned the corbel table on the exterior clerestory of Cluny III, substituting classically based corbels and narrow pilasters decorated with capitals, bases, and astragals (Fig. 102); however, the disappearance of the corbel table from the clerestory was only skin-deep. While decorating the high walls of the interior and

98. Malay, Notre-Dame, interior, apse, choir, and crossing, southern wall.

99. Cluny III, exterior, choir, southern aisle, detail of wall arch.

100. Cluny III, wooden model, prepared under the supervision of Kenneth Conant.

101. Tournus, Saint-Philibert, exterior, upper narthex, northern wall.

102. Cluny III, exterior, southern transept, northern bay, clerestory.

103. Cluny III, interior, southern transept, western wall, tower and northern bay, detail of squinch, transverse arch, and wall arches.

exterior with classical orders, masons also used relieving arches to re-inforce the wall supporting the weight of the vault. To ensure that these relieving arches support the continuous pressure from the enor-mous longitudinal barrel vault in the central vessel at Cluny, masons improved the construction of these small transverse arches. They added an extra row of arches, built the arches of ashlar, and coursed them to the adjacent responds and buttresses (Figs. 102, 103). The masons in effect formed the clerestory windows and second-story arcades into thick, stacked, transverse barrel vaults. As can be seen in both the nave

104. Paray-le-Monial, priory church, interior, northern nave and transept.

at Paray-le-Monial (Fig. 104) and the surviving transept at Cluny (see Figs. 102, 103), these vaults penetrate the nave wall and bolster the zone below the springing of the transverse arch.

In this structurally crucial location beneath the central barrel vault, the weight of the transverse arch descends into the wall, onto the exterior buttress behind the interior respond, and down the transverse walls above the aisle vaults (see Fig. 100). Linked to this vertical support system is an active horizontal one, made of a double row of transverse barrel vaults that brace the responds and buttresses from the

105. Cluny III, interior, southern transept, eastern wall, southern bay.

106. Cluny III, exterior, southern transept, southeast corner; (*a*) buttress extension.

107. Tournus, Saint-Philibert, interior, nave, northern aisle, two western bays.

sides. Together the two support systems form an interlinked ashlar skeleton that extends horizontally and vertically throughout each bay.

This network of linked horizontal arches and vertical supports exists in another form on the eastern wall of the southern transept. In the southern bay, a massive barrel vault exerts continuous lateral thrust at the level of the clerestory (Fig. 105). Inside, below the springing of the barrel vault, a giant relieving arch braces the wall, and outside, a pair of double concentric arches strengthens the wall above the clerestory (Fig. 106). On the sides of this bay, a skeleton of vertical responds and buttresses supports the interior wall arch. At the base of the arch, where the weight descends, the stones on the left course with the adjacent round and rectangular responds (see Fig. 105); on the right, the stones course into a small buttress that projects from the southern face of the transept (Fig. 106a). The masons distinguished this buttress from an adjacent larger one, which receives the weight from the transverse wall beneath the barrel vault.

Beneath the tower of the southern transept, a system of arches again is used to channel the continuous weight from a vault into the isolated supports in the corners of the bay. In this case, the pressure is exerted by a dome (see Fig. 105). Masons followed the same principles as the builders of the crossing at Chapaize (see Fig. 88) and the nave at Tournus (Fig. 107), who inserted diaphragm arches attached to semi-circular responds to support the continuous weight of a crossing dome and transverse barrel vaults. The masons at Cluny rested the two free-standing sides of the dome on diaphragm arches, whose springing is supported on massively projecting, perpendicularly intersecting, round and rectangular responds. On the southern side, a barrel vault braces the back of the diaphragm arch (see Fig. 105) and a giant, rectangular exterior buttress (visible on the right in Fig. 106) bolsters the spring-ing of this arch.

Masons rested the eastern and western sides of the dome on at-tached wall arches. Following the system of tower support found in lo-cal churches like those at Chapaize, Bray, and Laizé (see Figs. 88–90), they used wall arches on multiple levels to secure the walls. A giant *formeret* connects the lowest level, a less projecting order strengthens the wall below the dome, and vaulted squinches reinforce the corners of the crossing. In the adjacent bay on the northern side, a double row of small relieving arches abuts the springing of the giant *formeret* (see Fig. 103). In the bay on the southern side, a single, massive wall ar-cade secures this wall arch (see Fig. 105). In the transept of Cluny III, as in other late eleventh-century buildings in southern Burgundy, the brick-based system of arches braces the vault cell and stabilizes the wall surrounding the vault.

CHAPTER

7

The Pointed Arch and the Context of High Romanesque Architecture in Burgundy

 Two large conclusions so far have come from the discussion: (1) At the beginning of the eleventh century, in brick-based architecture throughout southern Europe, masons systematically pointed the webs and flattened the crossing of groin vaults. In contrast, in the churches built with ashlar in northern France at the same time, masons usually short-segmented the groins and kept the side of the webs unpointed. (2) Over the course of the eleventh century, masons in Burgundy refined this technology of pointed groin-vault construction and used it with sophisticated systems of arch support. These conclusions contradict the theory that masons in northern Europe first used the point at the end of the eleventh century in the context of barrel vaults in High Romanesque architecture in Burgundy.

In this chapter, I intend to expand these conclusions and show that Burgundian masons developed a distinctly local architecture based on the Italian brick tradition of building. To fashion their own forms, they depended on construction and vaulting techniques that had been used throughout the littoral from the beginning of the eleventh century. In particular, they exploited the skeletal qualities inherent in the wall arch, pointed web, and transverse arch of the First Romanesque groin vault. Burgundian masons focused on these special characteristics to create buildings that were high, wide, thin, spacious, and well lighted.

THE POINTED WEB IN LOMBARDY

It is not as if northern Italian masons sat on their hands: They also continued to exploit the traditional techniques of brick construction to create a distinctive form of architecture. Compared with their colleagues in Burgundy, however, masons in northern Italy stressed different aspects of the groin vault. They emphasized the round-headed features of semicircular arcades, *formerets,* and transverse arches.

In northern Italy, these round-headed features had existed alongside pointed webs in First Romanesque groin vaults (like the ones in the aisle at Lomello; see Fig. 18). By focusing on these features, and not on pointed webs, northern Italian masons created two major types of building. The first type continues an Early Christian and First Romanesque tradition in northern Italy. It has a wooden covered nave with round arches and arcades, as at Sant'Abbondio in Como and the cathedral at Modena.

In the second type, they expanded the kind of vertical articulation earlier northern Italian masons had preferred. At major buildings like Sant'Ambrogio at Milan and Santa Maria and San Sigismondo at Rivolta d'Adda (Fig. 108), the round arches and arcades in the nave are covered with a rib vault.[1] The rib usually is made of brick and formed into semicircular arches that resemble the adjacent *formeret* and transverse arches. This kind of arch creates vaults with square edges, semicircular openings, and a domical center.[2] These ribbed vaults become major points of focus, because each dome has a separate high crown and each dome unites a large double bay.

The combination of round-headed arches and domical vaults in these churches produces a visual experience different from the one at Cluny III (see Fig. 100). In northern Italy, masons explored the creative possibilities of the round arch, while in Burgundy masons focused on the other major ingredient of the groin vault: the pointed web. At sites like Cluny III, masons frequently extended the use of the point from groin webs to arcades, barrel vaults, and transverse arches. During the eleventh century in northern Italy, masons rarely explored these uses of the point; instead, they pursued the potential of the round parts of the groin vault. Over time, these experiments led to the widespread use of the rib, the dome, and alternating supports in square, double bays. Although they started from the same brick building tradition, northern

108. Rivolta d'Adda, Santa Maria and San Sigismondo, interior, nave and choir.

Italian and southern Burgundian masons emphasized different features that gave their architecture a distinct character.

These differences are not simply the result of separate preferences and traditions in the two regions. Once masons in northern Italy chose the round-headed formula, they could not simultaneously exploit it and the full potential of the pointed arch. A semicircular rib vault over a square bay creates a domical vault. A pointed transverse arch, or even a semicircular transverse arch, cannot reach the warped surfaces on top of this dome. Had they chosen a pointed transverse arch instead of a round-headed one, and had they stilted it and sprung it high instead of low – as at Rivolta d'Adda, where it begins at the midpoint of the nave wall (see Fig. 108) – even then, the masons could not have bridged the gap between the curved surface of the domical vault and the top of the transverse arch.

The issue here is twofold: Once they selected a domical rib, the masons could not exploit the flexibility inherent in a pointed transverse arch by raising the arch to reach the crown of the vault; and because they could not raise the transverse arch to reach the crown of each vault, they could not even the crown line among all vaults. An even crown line was necessary in order to run a longitudinal barrel vault down the nave. An even crown line probably was far from the minds of Lombard masons, however, who usually preferred low transverse arches and humped vaults that create isolated bays.

In all but the rarest examples, then, Italian masons chose a combination of features that all but excluded the use of a barrel vault with an even crown line in the central vessel of the nave.[3] In the major parts of buildings, they also rarely combined the two support types: continuous support, in the form of a barrel vault, and isolated support, in the form of the groin or rib vault. In contrast, in the nave of Burgundian churches, masons repeatedly combined these two structural solutions. Already by the beginning of the eleventh century, in the fully vaulted buildings at Tournus (see Fig. 14) and Chapaize, masons routinely mixed barrel and groin vaults, and later masons found new ways to unite these vault types

In summary, it can be said that northern Italian masons started from the same tradition of brick architecture as masons in southern Burgundy, but they developed a separate regional identity. Throughout most of the eleventh century, masons in Lombardy explored almost exclusively the side of First Romanesque architecture that emphasized groin-vaulted aisles, wooden-roofed naves, and low, round-headed transverse arches. These interests, focused as they were on the round arch, complemented the later introduction of semicircular ribs in domed churches. Once they pursued this direction, however, Italian masons in effect recused themselves from a whole line of vaulting research based on the pointed arch and barrel vault. In contrast, masons in Burgundy actively pursued the line of research based on the pointed arch and barrel vault, and it led them to explore unusual structures and aesthetics in buildings like Cluny III.

THE CONTEXT OF CLUNY

Nave of Saint-Philibert at Tournus

The nave of Saint-Philibert at Tournus (see Fig. 107) incorporates some of the same important features of local architecture that distinguish the lower narthex (see Fig. 14). Masons continued to use brick-shaped stones as the construction material, round piers with double-squared imposts as the support type, and the combination of barrel and groins as the covering for the vaulted interior. At the same time, they so changed the construction, structure, and appearance of these features that they transformed the basic *parti* of Bugundian First Romanesque architecture.

As they reviewed the options for vaulting the nave of Tournus, masons must have considered the standard barrel-vault solution that masons were using in the naves like those of Saint-Martin at Chapaize (see Fig. 35) and Saint-Martin-de-Laives.[4] In these structures, the corbel table in the clerestory and the groin vaults, *formerets,* and transverse arches in the aisles support the longitudinal barrel in the nave.[5] In the nave at Tournus, masons rethought and distilled this concept, in which relieving arches and the isolated webs of the groin vault absorb the continuous lateral pressure from the barrel vault. They increased the size and height of the asymmetrical vaults in the aisles; they also converted the barrel in the center of the nave from a longitudinal vault, which requires continuous lateral support, into transverse vaults on diaphragm arches, which require only point support. As a result of these changes, running corbel tables could be eliminated as relieving support from the exterior of the clerestory.

In the nave at Tournus, masons also altered the type of construction that had been used to build the lower narthex. Especially in the upper parts of the building, higher and wider brick-shaped stones create more solid supports. These stones also are finished more evenly, with less percussive blows and more superficial strokes. In the lower narthex, large carved blocks had not been used to reinforce isolated points of structural weakness. In the nave, in contrast, ashlar blocks buttress the structurally weak spots.

A sophisticated structure channels the weight from the central vault to the outside wall. Weight from the transverse barrels funnels through diaphragm arches to specific points high on the nave wall. From this location, three devices relay the weight directly to the groin webs in the aisles. At the top, masons secured the base of the diaphragm arches with large ashlar blocks, in the form of capitals and imposts, at the springing of the arches. As detailed in Chapter 4 (section "Asymmetrical Webs"), they then efficiently channeled the weight from these blocks to the outside walls by stilting the arches of the nave arcade and lowering the groin webs on the outside of the aisles (see Figs. 46, 47). Finally, they stabilized the pressure on the outside walls from these webs with the standard active cage of *formerets* and transverse arches, and expanded the width of the walls on the exterior with an extra plane of masonry at the point of impact (Fig. 109).

These structures in combination efficiently absorb the dead weight from the lateral barrels, and transfer it from the base of the diaphragm arches into the webs and expanded walls of the aisles. With this structural system in place, the stonework of the clerestory and pier supports could be reduced. Without risk, masons were able to minimize the wall beneath the vault to a fraction of the height of the elevation; open wide and high windows into this narrow story; and lengthen the piers and widen the distance between them, compared with the piers in the lower narthex.[6] These changes, in turn, allowed space and light to penetrate from the aisles into the central vessel.

The nave of Tournus often is considered a dead end because masons almost never repeated the structure of transverse barrel vaults on diaphragm arches. While it is true that masons abandoned the specific device of the transverse barrel vault as too complicated to build, they continued to explore the complex structure and visual arrangement that existed in the nave. The experiment at Tournus to isolate and relay vault pressure in the context of a thin, high, and open elevation had a lasting impact throughout the region.

Upper Narthex of Saint-Philibert at Tournus

To build the striking nave at Tournus, masons used the system of active arches and pointed groin webs that had been developed in transalpine churches, but they also applied this structure on a larger scale and in a broader context than before. They used the flexibility and strength of point supports to open the central wall, expand the height and width

109. Tournus, Saint-Philibert, exterior, nave, northern aisle, two western bays.

of the surrounding aisle spaces, and relay the weight of the lateral barrels to the aisle walls through points at the base of the diaphragm arches. The upper narthex was built as part of the nave, and, not unexpectedly, it repeats important features from the nave (see Figs. 65, 68).[7] Masons created a large clerestory; pronounced vertical nave responds; thin and layered wall planes; a narrow, steep central space covered by a barrel vault; and a tall arcade space, opening directly into a high lateral aisle space.

In the upper narthex, as in the nave, masons refined skeletal structure and point support within the context of a barrel vault and brick-based construction. In the upper narthex, unlike in the nave, they used a standard longitudinal barrel vault, but the results they achieved with this vault type were different from many of the earlier attempts to use the barrel. Both the upper narthex at Tournus and the Catalan church of Saint-Martin-du-Canigou (Fig. 110) combine a longitudinal barrel in the main vessel with longitudinal barrels in the aisles. The masons at Canigou, however, built the longitudinal barrel vault more simply: One instead of three sets of transverse arches and responds supports the central barrel vault; and in each aisle, a complete barrel, instead of a half barrel, relays the pressure from the central barrel to the outside walls. The central nave wall also does not rise above the height of the adjacent aisle vaults, and windows do not pierce the central vessel.

In the upper narthex at Tournus, longitudinal barrel vaults are used in a more complicated way than at Canigou. The builders decided to raise the central barrel above a high wall, puncture the wall with large openings, and reduce the aisle barrels to half vaults. To support this arrangement, in which the low aisle vaults do not directly support the high central vault, they had to find a special kind of structure: one that had both to absorb the immediate impact of the continuous horizontal pressure from the vault at the top of the wall, and transmit this pressure from the wall, across the aisle, to the perimeter of the church.

Three fundamentally different systems are used to stabilize this combination of longitudinal barrel vaults in the central and side aisles. At the level where the longitudinal barrel first hits the clerestory, they restrained the walls with wooden tie beams (see Fig. 71). In both the clerestory and aisles, to strengthen the area above the windows where the continuous pressure from the barrel vault hits the wall, they ran a horizontal row of relieving arches in the shape of a corbel table (see Figs. 13, 101).

As a third line of defense, they also inserted a system of isolated supports, similar to the combination of diaphragm arches and groin vaults in the nave. This system strengthens the wall beneath the vault, and it allows pressure from the vault to be isolated and transmitted through arches and vertical supports to the outside. In the eastern bay, the nave facade acts as a buttress to brace the longitudinal barrel vault. In the western bay, the narthex facade similarly buttresses the vault, wall arcade, and attached responds. In the aisles of this bay, two perpendicular walls descending beneath the facade tower support the isolated respond on each side of the nave.[8] In the middle bay, the central responds (on the left in Fig. 65) are enlarged and stiffened from behind by massive diaphragm arches (see Fig. 68). On the outside of the clerestory, a Lombard band, wider than the bands to either side of it, absorbs the pressure from these responds (see Fig. 101). Opposing relieving arches in the corbel table brace each side of this panel.

Once masons were able to stabilize pressure from the central vault with a combination of tie beams, relieving arches in corbel tables, and a skeleton of responds, arches, buttresses, and perpendicular walls, they could rethink the purpose and appearance of the elevation. They could explore wall effects that structurally were not available – and perhaps of minimal interest – to the masons who built the lower story

110. Saint-Martin-du-Canigou, abbey church, interior, nave, nineteenth-century prerestoration condition (author's detail photograph from restoration file, Caisse Nationale des Monuments Historiques).

of the narthex. At the beginning of the century in southern Burgundy, at eye level masons had often juxtaposed large, geometric parts and projected them from the wall to give sculptural focus to the repeated, undecorated, brick-shaped stones on the interior (see Figs. 35, 41). Over time, in buildings like the upper narthex at Tournus, masons took advantage of the armature on the inside and outside of the building to open and thin walls, expose wall planes, and punctuate the surface with decorative effects.

Masons noticeably reduced the relative thickness of the walls, as seen by a comparison of the arcades in the nave and upper narthex at Tournus (Fig. 111) with those in the nave at Chapaize. They also inserted arcade openings with ashlar decoration in the western bay of the upper narthex. These double-arcade openings not only interrupt the continuous coursing of the brick-shaped stones, they also punctuate the nave with large capitals supported by columns (Fig. 112).

111. Tournus, Saint-Philibert, interior, upper narthex, southern aisle and central vessel, facing west.

Masons opened and thinned the walls, but they still conceived and built them with the techniques of brick construction in mind. It would be a mistake to interpret the appearance of isolated ashlar decoration as an indication that the masons at Tournus began to gear up to produce large decorative blocks. In fact, most of the ashlar decoration was not intended for the location where it was used. Evidence from the capitals in the arcades of the upper narthex suggests that the masons who set the sculpture in place not only did not carve it, but they also had little if any close communication with those who had. For example, although the capital in the western arcade is carved only on three sides, masons set it in an arcade that is exposed all around (see Fig. 112). An even stronger indication of a change in intention between the masons who carved the sculptures and those who installed them, however, can be found in the capitals in the arcades on the eastern wall of the upper narthex (Fig. 113). In the northern arcade of this wall, the installers hacked the astragals off the capitals (Fig. 114), to give the bell a longer line; and in the southern arcade, they compensated for two capitals of different size by adjusting the height of the mortar bed and the circumference of the astragal on the columns beneath them.

112. Tournus, Saint-Philibert, interior, upper narthex, northern aisle, western bay, capital arcade.

113. Tournus, Saint-Philibert, interior, upper narthex, eastern wall, northern arcade.

Another more important indication of the intent of the designers is the way they used these capitals in the context of architecture. They made the arcades surrounding the sculpture of brick-shaped voussoirs and, in the manner of brick construction, protected these arcades with brick-shaped cover stones that rest on brick-shaped brackets (see Figs. 112, 113). They also extended the flat face of the arcades directly onto the face of brick-shaped imposts and continued this plane into square-

114. Tournus, Saint-Philibert, interior, upper narthex, eastern wall, northern arcade, capitals (detail of area shown in Fig. 113).

edged jambs, without the interruption of classical moldings. In these openings, they used ashlar only as spot decoration, and surrounded the opening with continuous brick coursing and articulation. The tentative use of ashlar capitals and columns shows the dominant position of brick-based construction in the upper narthex, and it reveals an important difference from the construction in the lower narthex, where no ashlar decoration of any kind is used.[9]

Perhaps the most striking example of the dominant position of masons who were trained in brick techniques over carvers who were trained in ashlar can be seen in the central bay of the wall separating the upper narthex from the nave (see Fig. 65). An apse originally occupied this space. In the portal to this apse, ashlar bases, capitals, and impost blocks are treated only as isolated forms within the surrounding brick-based wall (Fig. 115).

On this wall masons established a primary surface of brick-shaped stones and continued it flush with the plane of the carved socles, capitals, and figural blocks. They made no attempt to articulate this ashlar

115. Tournus, Saint-Philibert, interior, upper narthex,
eastern wall, central bay, portal, left jamb; (*a*) impost and
jamb stone; (*b*) cover stones above portal voussoirs.

carving, in the manner of contemporary northern French construction,
with horizontally projecting imposts or stringcourse moldings. Instead,
they preferred flush, continuous, vertical, square-edged surfaces, typical of southern brick-based construction.

  On the bottom of the portal, they extended the wall plane of brick-
shaped stones directly into the plane of the carved ashlar socles. In
the middle of the portal, between a foliate capital and a figural block,
they inserted a rectangular, brick-shaped impost. This impost looks like,
courses to, and is flush with the brick-based masonry adjacent to it

(Fig. 115a). The plane of this impost extends directly into the plane of the frame surrounding the figural block and the die and abacus on the upper part of the capital. Above the ashlar carving on top of the portal, the plane of the impost continues flush into the face of the brick-shaped cover stones (Fig. 115b). These cover stones, as do the cover stones in the double arcades adjacent to them, encircle and relieve the radiating brick-shaped stones of the portal arch.

The design of the upper narthex represents an important shift toward including northern vocabulary within the purely southern system of construction. The masons who erected the upper narthex, however, hardly were open to the full implications of northern building techniques, because they used ashlar decoration only in the context of brick-based wall and arch construction and articulation. It would take over a generation before southern Burgundian masons began to introduce complete ashlar structural systems within brick-based stone walls in the chevet of the abbey church at Anzy-le-Duc and the lower aisles of the eastern nave and chevet of Cluny III.

Masons made additional design changes between the lower and upper narthex. They took advantage of the isolated framework beneath the central vault to treat the nave wall as thin surface layers. In the nave and aisles, they corbeled the entire lower edge of the vault as a thin plane that projects from the vertical surface of the wall (see Figs. 66, 111). In the nave, square-edged brackets beneath a stringcourse molding with a brick profile, support this plane.

As they used more delicately revealed planes, masons became less interested in the massive juxtapositions that intrigued earlier builders in the region. This difference between the earlier and later taste can especially be seen in the articulation of the vault and supports. Instead of emphasizing the differences in geometric shapes at the point of articulation, as masons had done in the lower narthex (see Fig. 14), they extended the square-edged stringcourse molding beneath the plane of the vault directly into the stepped necking of the aisle piers (see Fig. 68).

On the exterior of the upper story of the narthex, masons showed a similar fascination with delicately exposed planes. On the lower story of the narthex, masons had projected narrow bands between wide stretches of blank wall. Within these differences in size and shape, the viewer recognizes the wider recessed portions of the wall (Fig. 116a),

116. Tournus, Saint Philibert, exterior, narthex, facade; (*a*) wall on ground floor; (*b*) Lombard band on ground floor; (*c*) band on upper floor; (*d*) wall on upper floor; (*e*) tower wall; (*f*) central wall.

as opposed to the narrower projecting bands (Fig. 116b), as the primary surface. In contrast, on the upper story, masons widened the bands in relation to the receded wall between them. Indeed, the bands have been expanded so much that the width of the projecting (Fig. 116c) and receding surfaces (Fig. 116d) is almost equal. The amount of receding and advancing masonry at the summit of the upper story wall also has been equalized. The area of projecting masonry, above the corbel tables in the two towers (Fig. 116e), balances the area of receding wall, below the rampant corbel tables in the center of the facade (Fig. 116f). As a result of these differences, between the upper and lower stories the relationship between the size of the receding and projecting walls changes. The viewer no longer sees the facade as a primary wall with secondary surface relief but instead recognizes both surfaces as equivalent planes.

Masons also took advantage of the isolated framework of responds, buttresses, and arches to increase the height, light, and space in the central vessel (see Figs. 65, 111). In the upper narthex, they raised the height of the longitudinal barrel well above the level of the half-barrel vaults in the aisles. In each bay, below the central barrel they punctured the nave wall with two large windows that descend more than half the distance between the vault and the arcades. They also opened light and space between the central vessel and the side aisles by making the arcade relatively high in relation to the piers; the circumference of the arcade arches dominates the short height of the round piers.

A comparison with other brick-based buildings underscores the unusual light, space, and proportions in the upper story at Tournus. In Catalonia at this time, masons also built fully vaulted churches, with a longitudinal central barrel and pronounced rectangular responds. In a small Catalan building like Fuilla or even a large structure like Sant Llorenç de Morunys, however, the openings of the arcade and windows usually are small in comparison with the amount of surface of the nave wall (see Fig. 10). The bays are relatively narrow and the supports relatively tall compared with these parts at Tournus, with the result that the circumference of the semicircular arches in the arcade does not reach as high in relation to the length of the piers. The majority of the interior elevation is devoted to an unbroken wall and usually is made from a single plane of continuously coursed, brick-shaped stones. In each bay only one narrow slit window descends less than half the distance between the vault and the arcade. In sum, these builders deemphasized the clerestory light and cross space in the interior, in favor of a flat wall that is broken only by small windows at the top and narrow arcades at the bottom.

In contrast, in the upper narthex at Tournus, masons emphasized the open windows and arcades in the nave wall. In each bay, they cut two large clerestory windows. They widened each window; splayed the jambs only slightly, so that the light from the outside almost fills the outline of the interior opening; and continued the opening down to the level of the springing of the aisle vault. As a result of this treatment, a large volume of light extends horizontally across the top of the nave elevation.

This handling of light contrasts with the treatment of light in most brick-based churches, even in the neighboring church at Chapaize (see Fig. 35). In this building, masons also built a nave with a longitudinal barrel and responds, but at the clerestory they depended on the relieving arches in the corbel table more than on an isolated framework of arches, buttress walls, and tie beams to support the weight from the vault.[10] They also responded to the pressure from the vault on the nave wall by minimizing clerestory openings. There is only one window per bay, and it is reduced to a small slit on the outside. The width of this opening on the inside is only a third the height, and the height is less than half the distance between the arcade and the vault.

In the central vessel of the upper narthex at Tournus, masons placed the large windows on a separate plane below the vault (Figs. 65, 111). Instead of aligning the surfaces of the wall and vault, they recessed the elevation slightly to the outside of the springing to allow more weight from the vault to pass through the heart, as opposed to the weaker inside, of the wall.[11] The masons took advantage of this efficient structure to build thinner walls. They also saved labor and materials by building a slightly narrower vault, because by corbeling the springers on either side of the nave, they could build a barrel with a shorter lateral span. In contrast, the masons at Chapaize made no attempt to recess the elevation below the vault or even to interrupt the wall plane with a horizontal molding. They simply extended the wall plane and curved the top of the windows directly into the springing of the vault (see Fig. 35).

The masons at Chapaize worked from the same local brick tradition as those who built the upper narthex at Tournus, but they emphasized different aspects of the interior. At Chapaize, isolated slit windows occupy a relatively small part of the elevation; the barrel vault extends directly into a flat vertical wall; and between the small arches on the bottom, the massive geometric shapes of the imposts, responds, and piers collide. The focus is very different in the upper narthex at Tournus, where masons horizontally illuminated the interior with large double clerestory windows and complemented this light with a thin recessed wall, a high and wide nave arcade, and ashlar capitals, imposts, brackets, and voussoirs around points of stress.

To complement the high and well-lit space of the central vessel, masons also emphasized the horizontal space between the nave and the aisles. At Chapaize, the arch of the arcade is small in relation to the height of the wall and piers, and it springs at a relatively low level. In the upper narthex at Tournus, in contrast, masons raised the height of the arcade arches and side-aisle vaults in relation to the height of the piers and nave wall (see Figs. 65, 68). As a result, the viewer gets the impression of more open lateral space between the nave and aisles (see Fig. 111) than at Chapaize or in the lower narthex at Tournus (see Fig. 14).

In the lower narthex, masons had made the radius of the arcade arches small, about a third the height of the piers; the height of the piers tall, almost twice the length of the piers in the upstairs chapel; and the circumference of the piers wide, almost the same dimensions as the space between them in the aisles. At eye level the viewer primarily encounters massive round piers separated by dark spaces, unilluminated by windows in the central vessel.

In the upper narthex, masons narrowed the mass of the piers. They also lowered their height to almost equal the radius of the arches between them, with the result that the nave arcade springs below eye level. With the aid of light from a large clerestory, the visitor sees straight through the arcades to the vaulted aisle, without confronting wide piers at eye level.

The masons also used the transverse arches and vaults inside the side aisles to enhance the effect of space within and between the aisles. A skeleton of transverse arches and diaphragm walls divides the bays of the side aisles. To allow more light and space to continue longitudinally, they increased the height of the transverse arches by stilting them (see Fig. 68). Only in each eastern bay – where the transverse arch is attached to the wall, and therefore does not divide the aisle space – did they not stilt the arch.[12]

To emphasize the continuous space between the nave and side aisles, the masons also manipulated the type and placement of the side-aisle vaults. They selected half-barrel vaults, placed them longitudinally, and rested the peaks of these vaults high above the nave arcades. This kind of vault allows an unimpeded view from the central vessel into the side aisles. The masons also increased the space behind the nave wall by horizontally extending the peak of the half barrels beyond the crown line.

Another reason they used these horizontal extensions was to enhance the light and improve the structure of the building. If the masons could horizontally extend the top of a small half-barrel vault,
instead of building a larger, and therefore higher, half-barrel vault, they
could make the clerestory windows descend without having them
overlap the peak of the aisle vaults. The advantage of this arrangement
is that the more the windows increase in size by extending lower, the
more light enters the nave. To cover the same width in the aisle, an
alternative would have been to prolong downward the peak of a smaller half-barrel vault into a more complete circle segment. Instead, they
expanded the width of the aisle by horizontally projecting the top of
a larger quarter circle. Extending the vault in this manner at its peak
allowed them to transfer weight more directly – and therefore more
efficiently – from the central barrel vault, through the nave wall, to
the exterior of the side aisle.

In the aisles of the lower narthex, masons had used complete semicircular barrel vaults: They placed them transversally and dropped the
springing below the necking of the piers (see Fig. 14). This placement
of the barrel vaults creates a different visual impression than in the
upper narthex. The humped shape of the lateral barrels and the low
springing of the unstilted transverse arches produce bays that are interrupted and enclosed. From the central vessel, the viewer does not see
an open and continuous aisle space.

In the upper narthex (see Figs. 65, 68), viewers experience a world
that is different from the open space between elongated piers in the
nave (see Fig. 107). They see small piers in the main vessel, intimate
proportions in the aisles, and uneven space between the central and
side aisles. Visitors find the experience in both parts of the building similar, however, in that once they enter the relatively narrow and steep
confines of the central vessel, they encounter a large volume of space
and light (see Fig. 111). In this sense, in the nave and upper narthex
at Tournus masons created an environment different from that found
in any other contemporary, barrel-vaulted church.

Saint-Hippolyte and Cluny III

When masons contemplated building Cluny III, they had only to turn
to the nave at Tournus for a system of isolated supports with a high

barrel vault in the central vessel. As impressed as they must have been by this system, however, they nevertheless did not opt for a vaulting solution with transverse barrel vaults.[13] They probably recognized that the height, space, and light gained by using transverse barrels in the central space did not justify the drawbacks in design, construction, and structure.

Aesthetically, transverse barrel vaults, and the diaphragm arches that support them, interrupt the space and walls of the interior. The humped profile of each barrel vault breaks the continuous crown line, and the spandrel wall in each diaphragm arch obstructs the continuous flat surface of the elevation.

A transverse barrel vault is also difficult to build. In the nave at Tournus, the diaphragm arch below every transverse barrel supports only a fraction of the weight from the vault. This diaphragm arch absorbs the dead weight from the vault, as opposed to the pressure exerted by the thrust, and diverts it laterally to a point at the base of the arcade spandrel in the elevation. The diaphragm arch principally acts as a contact point and relay station for the weight from the barrel vaults that oppose each other on either side of every arch. The diaphragm arch stabilizes this pressure, coming from opposite directions, before passing it, from one vault to the next, down the nave. To build a transverse barrel in each bay, then, masons faced a double problem: As they pondered how to deal with the dead weight that descends laterally down the diaphragm arch to the nave wall, they had to worry about the greater pressure, relayed in a longitudinal direction, from the previously finished vault.[14]

At Cluny, masons avoided these problems by rejecting transverse barrels, choosing instead to vault the central vessel with a longitudinal barrel vault. This type of vault was common in the nave of brick-based architecture in Burgundy, and by the end of the eleventh century, masons had found ways to improve its structure. To enable the weight of the vault to descend more vertically, and therefore more efficiently, they pointed the barrel, as well as the arcades and transverse arches beneath it.

As seen in the ruined cross section of the Cluniac abbey church at Saint-Hippolyte, they also fine-tuned the system that transfers the weight from the barrel vault in the nave to the groin vault in the aisles (Figs. 117, 118). This church had one of the largest naves with a longi-

117. Saint-Hippolyte, priory church, interior, nave (author's detail photograph from restoration file, Caisse Nationale des Monuments Historiques).

tudinally pointed barrel vault in the Mâconnais. (The abbey is located only a short distance north of Cluny.)[15]

The masons who built Saint-Hippolyte followed the local tradition of brick-based stone construction. The walls, windows, jambs, and even archivolts and transverse arches are built with bricklike stones (Figs. 119, 120).[16] Masons often worked the surface of these stones with irregular percussive strokes, but they also used techniques that indicate they were active at the end of the eleventh century. At times they finished the surface with relatively even and superficial blade strokes, extended the length of the stones beyond the normal brick size, and cut the edges of the blocks into straight edges.

Saint-Hippolyte has much in common with Cluny III, where masons created similar massing, space, and articulation. They based these features ultimately, if not directly, on a local building like the upper narthex at Tournus. At Saint-Hippolyte and Cluny III, masons made the central vessel extremely narrow compared with the length of the nave (see Figs. 100, 117), and covered this narrow shape with an un-

118. Saint-Hippolyte, priory church, interior, nave, southern aisle (author's detail photograph from restoration file, Caisse Nationale des Monuments Historiques); (*a*) narrow extended base beneath corbeled portion of vault; (*b*) flattened web top; (*c*) thin spandrels covering high and flat springing of vault; (*d*) horizontally coursed stones in corbel vault; (*e*) outside face of wall at base of second story.

usually high space. In these buildings, they encouraged the passage of light and space between the nave and aisles in a number of ways. They extended the height of the arcades and sprang the groin vaults from a high point in the aisles (see Figs. 44, 63). They built the webs of the groins with steep and relatively flat arrises; in the central aisle, they took advantage of the flattened shape of these arrises to mask the ex-

119. Saint-Hippolyte, priory church, interior, nave at crossing, detail of ruined central vault and elevation.

posed sides of the webs with narrow spandrels. They also arranged the side aisles into shallow, longitudinal bays that emphasize the continuity of space between the vessels (see Fig. 118).

In the nave at Saint-Hippolyte, masons made the height of the nave-arcade opening more than the combined height of the nave wall and vault. This opening allows the space in the narrow and high central vessel to continue directly into the lateral space of the aisles. Masons also increased the continuity of space from the central vessel to the side aisle by raising the springing of the aisle vault to a level above three-quarters of the height of the aisle wall (see Figs. 117, 118a).

120. Saint-Hippolyte, priory church, interior, nave, southern aisle, ruined vaults; (*a*) brick-shaped stones in corbeled portion of vault course between groin webs.

They also opened the lateral space by narrowing the base of the corbeled groin into a thin strip (see Fig. 118a) and bending the true vault into flat web segments (see Fig. 118b). This arrangement avoids the kind of projecting springers at the bottom of the vault and steeply curved arrises at the top that interrupt the line of sight between the central and side aisles. It also allows for an arcade with a delicate arch. Masons covered the back side of the vaults with spandrels that are thinner and descend less far on the elevation (see Fig. 118c) than if the corbels and webs had been fully curved. Once they made the arcade tall, the groin vault high and flat, and the spandrels thin, they took the next step and reduced the wall – the only solid remaining below the barrel vault – to less than half the height of the arcades (see Fig. 117). They also opened this wall to light. Prerestoration photographs show that at the center of every bay they penetrated this solid horizontal strip with a wide window that descends almost to the peak of each arcade.[17]

At Saint-Hippolyte, masons explored another aspect of building that masons had pursued on the inside and outside of the upper narthex at Tournus: They widened the traditional brick device of the Lombard band into a wall plane. They distinguished themselves from the masons at Tournus, however, by exploring these planar effects with less

121. Saint-Hippolyte, priory church, exterior, chevet; (*a*) reveal on side wall of choir; (*b*) reveal on eastern wall of choir; (*c*) band on apse.

traditional brick vocabulary, like corbel tables and sawtooth string-course moldings.

Inside and outside the chevet at Saint-Hippolyte, builders replaced these traditional brick devices by wall planes with tiny, vertically continuous reveals. They made the vertical reveals of the wall and windows on the side of the choir (Fig. 121a) analogous to the reveal of the eastern wall of the choir (Fig. 121b) and the reveals of the wide bands between the windows of the apse. Inside the chevet, the same kind of square-edged vertical reveals are used to expose the planes of the wall (Fig. 122). The depth of the reveal in the arcade around the windows in the apse and choir (Fig. 122a) is the same size as the face of the voussoirs (Fig. 122b) surrounding these openings. As a result of these similarities, the arcades and window archivolts look alike. In addition, the dimensions of the vertical square edges beneath these arches are identical with the dimensions of the reveals that expose the side of the apse (Fig. 122c). Masons emphasized the effect of layered planes by extending the face of the reveals into the broader surface areas of the apse. They extended the face of the arcade (Fig. 122d) directly into the surface of the half-domed vault; the face of the window voussoirs directly into a panel beneath the window openings (Fig. 122e); and the face of the reveal (Fig. 122c) on the side of the curved apse wall directly overhead into a vertical plane with a window (Fig. 122f).

At Saint-Hippolyte, not only did masons arrange the space, proportions, and wall surfaces in the manner of the upper chapel at Tournus, they also constructed the vaults with local brick-building techniques. At the base of the groin vaults (the lower 25 percent of the web), brick-shaped stones course horizontally into corbel vaults (see Fig. 120), and between adjacent webs they extend without interruption into the hearting of the aisle walls (Fig. 120a). These coursed stones support the weight from the springing of the true vaults in the aisles.

In the aisles, the masons constructed the top three-quarters of the groin webs as true vaults (see Figs. 44, 118b). They built these webs from a row of radially laid, brick-shaped stones that spring above the horizontally coursed stones in the corbel base (Fig. 118d). The barrel vault in the main vessel also is pared to the thickness of one radially placed brick (see Fig. 119). Reducing the weight of these vaults allowed masons to open large windows and reduce the thickness of supporting corbels, piers, and walls.

122. Saint-Hippolyte, priory church, interior, choir and apse; (*a*) reveal in arcade around window; (*b*) face of window voussoirs; (*c*) reveal on side of apse; (*d*) half dome; (*e*) panel beneath window; (*f*) vertical plane above apse reveal.

123. Saint-Hippolyte, priory church, interior, nave, northern aisle, western bay; (*a*) horizontally laid brick-shaped stones above extrados of transverse arch.

To build groin vaults in the aisles, they rested the radially laid stones of the webs on horizontally placed filler stones (Fig. 123a) which are arranged lengthwise above stilted transverse arches. The filler stones work in combination with the stilted transverse arch to boost the height of the longitudinal webs in relation to the diagonal groins. Together they serve, in the manner of southern brick construction, to even the crown line of the vaults in the aisle. Above this crown, masons used the single row of radially laid stones of the true vaults to support the horizontal courses of the second-story floor (see Fig. 117).

The masons at Saint-Hippolyte also applied the integrated vaulting techniques of earlier masons who practiced brick-based architecture in Burgundy. Both continuous horizontal and isolated vertical supports are used to absorb the weight from the central vault and direct it to the outside aisle walls. Between the bottom of the central barrel and the top of the aisle groins, masons widened the exterior face of the nave by extending the lower courses of the wall almost to the crown of the aisle vault (see Figs. 118e, 119). The added courses at the base of the wall absorb the weight from springing of the barrel and channel it directly to the outside webs and aisle walls.

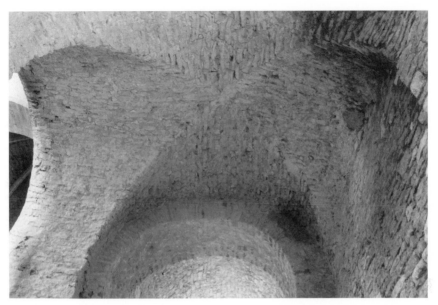

124. Gigny, abbey church, interior, nave, southern aisle, eastern bay, groin vault.

Masons also used a variant on the asymmetrical webs that masons had deployed in the aisles of the nave at Tournus. This type of web maximizes the ability of the groin vault to transfer the continuous weight from the longitudinal barrel in the nave to the separate webs on the outside of the aisles. The arrises on the outside of the aisles are canted in a more vertical, and thus more structurally efficient, angle than the arrises on the inside of the aisle (see Fig. 44). The size of the outside web also is reduced, making it more compact and stable than the webs on the interior of the aisles. To improve further the efficiency of this web, they lowered its height by eliminating the *formeret* beneath. The web is laid directly on a recessed lip that courses to the masonry inside the wall (see Fig. 120). As in the vaults in the cloister and nave aisles at Tournus and in the nave aisle at Cluny, webs that are lower on the outside than on the inside increase the angle of descent and improve the structural efficiency of the groin vault.

For almost a century, masons had experimented with this kind of asymmetrical vault in brick-based architecture in the region of Cluny. In the Jura, in the Cluniac abbey church at Gigny, the groin vaults in the southeastern aisle have asymmetrical webs with steep outside arrises (Fig. 124), which cross outside the center of the transverse arch.

These asymmetrical features improve structure by making the outside web more compact and vertical and by channeling the weight from the central vessel more directly to the aisle wall.[18] At both Gigny and Saint-Hippolyte, the structural efficiency of this type of web allowed masons to dispense with the added brace of *formerets* on the walls.

Tournus, Saint-Hippolyte, and the Context of Cluny III

At the beginning of the eleventh century, in the nave of Saint-Philibert at Tournus, masons followed local tradition by combining barrel and groin vaults. They also introduced a new variant by placing the barrels transversely in the central vessel, but this device had aesthetic and constructional disadvantages that inspired few copies. Placing barrel vaults crosswise did, however, make possible a new combination of light, space, and skeletal construction. In southern Burgundy, these features came to dominate important eleventh-century churches associated with Cluny.[19]

In the nave of Cluny III (see Figs. 1, 100), masons combined the key elements of the structure and elevation from the nave at Tournus (see Fig. 107). These features include a large clerestory opening; thin, layered wall planes; a small nave wall; a system of isolated supports that transfer weight from the central vessel via groin webs to the aisles; a narrow, steep central space covered by a barrel vault; and enormously tall arcades, opening directly onto wide and high lateral aisle spaces. Masons in both churches created a nave elevation that is open for two-thirds of its height on the bottom and for almost half its width at the top, and solid for only a short section in between.

To help achieve these results, in the transept at Cluny III masons used the local system of horizontal relieving arches – in the form of *formerets,* transverse arches, and clerestory arches – to strengthen the inside of walls and stabilize the pressure from vaults (see Chapter 6, section "Mazille, Malay, and Cluny III"). The nave of Cluny III no longer exists, but it probably combined the same structural principles as in the transept. It coupled a continuous horizontal barrel vault and clerestory arcade to a system of transverse arches and giant, isolated, vertical supports. The evidence for this hypothesis is of two kinds. The first is seventeenth- and eighteenth-century drawings and engravings of the building. The second type of evidence is based on the analogy

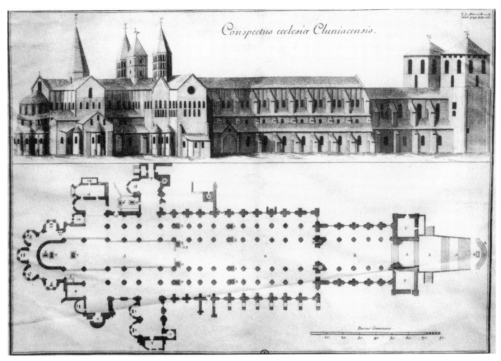

125. Cluny III, exterior view and plan, P. F. Giffart, between 1685 and 1713.

of the destroyed nave with surviving parts of the mother church, and with the choir of the priory church at Paray-le-Monial that was modeled on Cluny III.[20]

Before Cluny III was dynamited and disassembled at the beginning of the nineteenth century, artists had illustrated the interior and exterior of the nave. These detailed renderings show that masons learned from the structure at buildings like the upper narthex at Tournus. To strengthen the barrel vault, at Tournus masons had increased the size of the central respond and added an extra-wide Lombard band behind it (see Figs. 65, 101). Similarly, in each bay of the nave at Cluny, masons created isolated supports that girdle the upper two stories. On the upper two stories of the interior, to help absorb the weight from each transverse arch at the springing of the vault, they projected a massive colonnette and on each side flanked it with a *dosseret* (see Figs. 1, 100). They braced the reverse side of these interior responds with massive, projecting exterior buttresses, separated by two narrow and flat pilasters (Fig. 125; the flying buttresses were added later).[21]

126. Cluny III, nave, interior, bay six, southern outside aisle, wall above transverse arch.

In the nave at Cluny, as in the upper narthex at Tournus, at a high level in the elevation, the weight from the barrel vault and transverse arch is channeled outside the building. This transfer is accomplished through a system of isolated supports made of interior responds, rampant walls, and exterior buttresses. Rampant walls, perpendicular to the elevation, and groin vaults, cascading on two levels, relieve the weight from the support bundles inside the nave (see Fig. 100). Under the roofs of both aisles (Fig. 126), the weight from the exterior clerestory buttresses diagonally descends through these walls into thick rubble-filled ashlar buttresses (Fig. 127) on deep spur foundations.[22] Between these buttresses, *formerets* on the inside and relieving arches on the outside (see Fig. 99) stabilize the high aisle wall and brace the responds and buttresses that receive pressure from the upper stories. At Cluny, this system that combines continuous horizontal and isolated vertical support goes back to experiments with relieving arches and barrel and groin vaults in the nave and narthex of Tournus. These large-scale experiments that link horizontal and vertical structure distinguish southern Burgundian architecture from the brick-based architecture in northern Italy.

The surviving transept of Cluny III and the central vessel of Paray-le-Monial (see Fig. 104) provide further evidence that at spots high on the elevation of the mother church, masons combined horizontal and

127. Cluny III, exterior, nave, south-ern aisle, bay six, buttress during reconstruction in 1996.

isolated vertical support to redirect the weight from the vault to but-tresses. On the upper stories, each massive colonnette courses with the adjacent supports. The large ashlar blocks in the colonnettes course not only with the masonry in the rectangular responds, on the sides of the colonnettes, but also with the masonry in the buttresses, behind the colonnettes. The colonnettes on the upper two stories serve an impor-tant structural purpose: They are part of a coursed skeleton that con-nects the inside and outside of the building. Together, the colonnettes and responds function as an enormous support bundle that absorbs weight from the vault and transverse arch overhead, as well as from the relieving arches on each side, and transmits it directly to a buttress on the exterior.

This bundle was not left as an isolated point of pressure on the el-evation. Instead, following the tradition of corbeled relieving tables, masons braced either side of the bundle with three vaulted window arcades made of ashlar voussoirs (see Figs. 100, 103). On the upper story they made these arcades of solid ashlar and coursed the beds into exterior buttresses. In so doing, they created a continuous horizontal skeleton of transverse vaults that structurally join the massive vertical responds and buttresses.[23]

Masons sought to ensure that the clerestory windows and responds remained stable as weight from the central vault descended diagonally through them. To achieve this end, in the second story of each bay they repeated the three lateral vaults that are used on the third story, retaining their deep vaults while reducing the double columns and projecting billet molding to pilasters and a recessed horseshoe molding.

Because the diagonal roof covering the groin vaults over the inside aisle leans directly against the second story of the main vessel, at this level no light can directly reach the interior of the church (see Fig. 100). Aware of the lack of outside light, on the second story of the nave as well as the choir, masons left the two side arcades blind; they opened only the central arcade, to illuminate with reflected interior light the crawl space below the aisle roof. In the transepts, no aisles, and therefore no crawl spaces above the aisles, surround the central vessel; so on the second story of the transepts all the arcades are blind (see Fig. 103). By closing most of the second-story arcades, masons followed the tradition of earlier builders who strengthened the transverse vaults in the corbel table by filling them in. Taking advantage of the double row of six relieving arches per bay, masons created a skeleton by penetrating the top story and reducing the intermediary story to a narrow band of deep blind arcades.[24]

By using a double row of ashlar transverse barrels on the upper two stories to stabilize the wall carrying weight from the vault, masons adapted and substantially improved the relieving corbel system that had been used earlier in Burgundy. By the time of Cluny III, masons also changed other brick-based structures. In particular, they improved barrel vaulting to a point at which they could place the transverse barrels well below the springing of the longitudinal barrel – on a level even with the clerestory windows – a position relatively lower than that of most corbel tables. Lowering the relieving arches below the loaded haunches and the springing of the vault allowed them to combine light from the clerestory with the lateral support system. It has sometimes been suggested that the building structure was weakened by opening a large clerestory exactly where the continuous pressure from the barrel hits the wall.[25] In reality, by opening a series of transverse barrel vaults derived from the century-old system of corbel tables, masons achieved the opposite effect: They lightened and strengthened the clerestory wall.

To reduce the pressure on the transverse barrels in the wall, masons tried to decrease the width of the longitudinal barrel vault and increase its vertical angle of penetration. In the brick-derived upper narthex at Tournus, masons had corbeled the springing of the barrel over the central vessel, pushing the vault inside and realigning the diagonal pressure from the vault so that it hits a lower spot on the elevation. At Cluny, masons achieved the same benefits by cantilevering the vault on corbeled arcades (see Figs. 100, 103). In the clerestory of each bay of the three-story elevation, they cantilevered the inside plane of the barrel vault above a billet molding on three corbeled arcades. The result resembles the three giant corbel tables that support the vault in the Cluniac chapel at Berzé-la-Ville. On the exterior, they widened the base of the three-story wall to absorb the pressure diagonally exerted by the barrel vault (see Fig. 100). Whereas on the interior they projected the third story over the lower stories, on the exterior they reversed the profile by projecting the second story beyond the plane of the clerestory. In the aisles of the upper narthex at Tournus masons had not only straightened the vault springing to an almost vertical angle, they had also extended the crown into a straight, albeit horizontal, angle. These vaults were much more efficient than half- or quarter-circle barrels, whose low angle requires thick lateral walls to support the pressure of the vault. Having witnessed the improved efficiency of small barrel vaults like these in an important local building at Tournus, the masons who built the grandiose barrels in the nave and transept of Cluny III extended the crown of the vault into a point and straightened its springing to approach a vertical angle.[26]

By combining structural improvements at Cluny III, masons could place relieving arcades lower in the elevation, and could void and thin the interior wall on all levels. The structural synthesis at Cluny includes

1. redirecting the weight from the barrel into a more vertical direction by corbeling the vault and straightening its crown and springing;

2. concentrating the support beneath the vault by applying ashlar buttresses and responds to the nave wall; and
3. increasing the lateral support around the vault by stacking a double row of ashlar arcades beneath its springing.

For the ashlar framing and support needed to achieve this complex and monumental solution, masons turned to sources outside the brick tradition; but for other essential components – corbeling and straightening the barrel vault and girdling it with arcades – they relied upon the sophisticated, local, brick-based system of lateral support. Masons recognized that, by joining the clerestory and transverse barrels into one massive structure, they could improve the traditional lateral support and build higher walls, more open to light and space. The stability of this structure made it possible to lighten the whole upper story; to bring the three clerestory windows well below the springing of the barrel vault; to increase the arcade height – the other voided area in the elevation – to more than half the height of the elevation; and to penetrate the center arch of the middle story in order to create a novel, three-story, skeletal elevation.[27]

CONCLUSION

At Cluny and Paray-le-Monial masons not only used the traditional system of isolated supports and relieving arches but also modified and expanded it. They improved the traditional semicircular longitudinal barrel by stilting and pointing it. They also used a network of ashlar supports to improve structure at isolated points of stress. At Tournus, masons had restricted ashlar to spots, like arcades and diaphragm arches, where stress concentrates. At Cluny, masons combined ashlar responds on the inside, ashlar buttresses on the outside, and ashlar lateral barrel vaults on two stories in between.[28]

They used this combination of new and old technology to expand the type of elevation, light, and space that at Tournus masons had achieved with brick-based masonry, barrel vaults, and isolated vertical supports. In the upper narthex and nave of Tournus, masons had experimented with a new formula that included a large clerestory, a small nave wall, and tall arcades that open directly into wide and high lateral aisle spaces. Without fear of a vault collapse, at Cluny masons further raised the bottom story with an enormously high, pointed arcade, opened the top story with three giant windows per bay, and topped this stream of light with a pitched and pointed barrel vault.[29] They pierced the only solid wall left – a narrow, second-story blind arcade – with an opening in the middle of each bay and peeled back the surface on the sides. Even as they added classical vocabulary and ashlar details, they also reduced the surface to thin layers. They expanded the simple, square-edged planes that dominate the upper narthex of Tournus and exposed different kinds of surface elements – like blind arcades, corner responds, and column arcades – as a series of narrow, delicate, square-edged reveals.

Conclusion

Documents do not describe in detail either the people who built the early eleventh-century architecture in southern Europe or the circumstances under which they worked. To compensate for a lack of documentary knowledge and evidence, I carefully examined churches to understand how masons put them together.

The goal has been an integrated approach to an almost purely visual subject. To achieve this goal, I attempted to "control" conclusions about the creative process by placing them in a limited context of time and space. It is risky to draw conclusions about intent based on isolated works of art, and therefore, without diminishing the uniqueness of each building, I set out to explore the ambitions of workers within two distinct but overlapping traditions. In Lombardy, masons who used bricks established a pattern of building at the beginning of the eleventh century; and in Burgundy, over the course of the eleventh century, masons modified and expanded this tradition.

To fathom how these artisans thought and worked, I approached each major building as a whole, hoping to make connections among physical properties of building, formal relationships within a design, and decisions based on craftsmanship and long-standing workshop practices. In other words, I searched for clues about creation and execution by balancing the study of construction and structure with an investigation of aesthetics and labor. This concrete but intertwined approach may offer a new paradigm for discussing structural issues in medieval architecture.

More often than not, in the past, medieval vaulting has been isolated as a subject and used primarily to understand the sources of the Gothic style. Questions of vaulting have been treated as typological issues – boiled down to such questions as the origin of the rib vault and the development of the flying buttress; analyzed as part of an evolutionary process, like the transition from the barrel to the rib vault; discussed without adequately considering construction, articulation, and decoration; or studied apart from the specific contexts of labor and masonry, as found in the Lombard brick-based tradition.

The result has been a narrow approach that depreciates the contribution of southern European architecture at the turn of the eleventh century in comparison with the accomplishment of the architecture that succeeded it. In the case of buildings in Burgundy, scholars have described brick-based architecture around the year 1000 as primitive and unprogressive, and used it as a foil to establish the original and nonlocal character of Cluniac structures that "replaced" it.

My integrated approach that balances issues of structure, construction, and aesthetics led to many discoveries about the character of architecture at the beginning of the eleventh century. Masons who built the earliest brick-based churches in southern Europe did not focus only on thick walls with continuous weight and superficial banded decoration. They also combined the isolated support of pointed webs in groin vaults, a framework of *formerets,* transverse arches, and nave arcades that stabilize the vaults, and internal relieving arches in adjacent walls to create a flexible, complicated, and refined architecture. The discovery of these skeletal qualities suggests that the Lombard system of building no longer should be branded as rudimentary and folkloric, or divorced from the progressive and sophisticated developments of later Romanesque and Gothic architecture.

In Burgundy masons took this Lombard system and placed their own stamp on it. In particular, they expanded the Lombard basilica interior, based on the Early Christian model that has a continuously flat and unvaulted central nave. Early-eleventh-century brick-based Burgundian buildings usually have a vertically linked system of arches, responds, and supports; they usually also are fully vaulted, requiring isolated support for groin vaults and continuous support for barrel vaults. To brace these complicated vaults, masons used Lombard re-lieving corbel tables in combination with isolated supports and point-ed asymmetrical webs. In these buildings they combined brick-shaped stones as the construction material, round piers with double-squared or trapezoidal imposts as the support type, pronounced responds as the articulating members, and the combination of barrel and groins as the vaults. Using this new combination of construction, structure, and design, in the nave and upper narthex of Saint-Philibert at Tournus masons transformed the standard Lombard type of elevation. They in-troduced elongated arcades, spots of ashlar decoration, high and wide spaces, large clerestory windows, and a vertical articulation that joined vault, wall, and supports.

The new and specific information about the progressive character of international and local brick-based architecture provided an oppor-tunity to reevaluate High Romanesque buildings in Burgundy. I applied the same methods to these buildings, and was able to make a precise and balanced interpretation of their complex features and to clarify the origins and originality of the design of Cluny III. The examination of the aisle bays in the mother church, for example, shows that masons applied the Lombard system of vaulting that had been refined locally. They inserted the brick-based system of corbeling, webbing, and fram-ing. They also updated this structure by expanding the use of ashlar and pointed-arch construction in the arches surrounding the vault. In these aisles, as elsewhere in the church, masons took advantage of the added strength from this updated system to increase light, space, thin-ness, and decoration.

These insights into the cause and character of designs at buildings like Farges, Saint-Hippolyte, and Cluny III also challenge our under-standing of High Romanesque as a historical concept. Artistic decisions during that time can now be seen as less abstract, dramatic, and sim-ple, and more practical, delicate, and complicated. The appearance of these Burgundian churches represents not so much a revolution or stylistic break, as heretofore thought, as a surviving, yet energetically changing, system of building. Intellectual monks and globetrotting artists were not needed to rescue an impoverished local tradition, with a limited folkloric perspective, by synthesizing contemporary European achievements into a novel statement. Masons at the end of the elev-enth century did not so much introduce a new type of design, stage of development, or level of artistic understanding, as continue, refine, and enrich the complex and sophisticated local artistic traditions. By stating this new position, I do not mean to detract from the originality and importance of the mother church – its enormous scale, unique appearance, and specific decoration set it apart – or to diminish the significance of changes that occurred over thirty years between the construction of the eastern aisles and west facade. I intend simply to give a specific context and meaning to the creativity in southern Burgundy at the end of the eleventh century.

Finally, the discovery of the context for the pointed arch suggests new ways of approaching architecture in many periods besides the Romanesque. The often-seamless connection among structure, construction, and design opens a window into the creative process, particularly for buildings that are not well documented. Seeing the issue of vaulting as more than a structural problem also challenges some broad beliefs about the nature of change in architecture. The evidence shows that devices like the pointed arch did not appear in northern France at the turn of the twelfth century, as the science of building "evolved" from seemingly less sophisticated forms, like the barrel vault, with its restrictive continuous lateral pressure, to seemingly more sophisticated ones, like the groin or rib vault, with its narrow point support. Architectural history, presented in this way – as a series of steady structural improvements – limits our understanding of individual buildings and simplifies the context of creation and the process of change.[1]

Notes

INTRODUCTION

1. In contrast, a *pointed arch* often is defined as two curves with equal radii meeting at the top, and an *ellipse* is defined as the path of a point that moves so that the sum of its distances from two fixed points, the foci, is constant. See René Chappuis, "Utilisation du tracé ovale dans l'architecture des églises romanes," *Bulletin monumental* 134, 1976, 7–36.

2. Kenneth John Conant, *Carolingian and Romanesque Architecture 800 to 1200*, Baltimore, 1959.

3. Josep Puig i Cadafalch, *La Géographie et les origines du premier art roman*, Paris, 1935.

4. A few studies on this subject appeared in the first part of the twentieth century. See Arthur Kingsley Porter, *The Construction of Lombard and Gothic Vaults*, New Haven, 1911; Edmond Malo, "Les Voûtes de la chapelle haute de l'église abbatiale de Tournus," *Bulletin monumental* 98, 1939, 73–84; more recently, see Malcolm Thurlby, "Observations on Romanesque and Gothic Vault Construction," *Arris* 6, 1995, 22–9. The study of wall construction, as opposed to vaulting and articulation, is an active field of research in France. See Nicolas Reveyron, "Les Nouvelles Approches de l'architecture médiévale," *Dossiers d'archéologie* 251, 2000, 2–5. Günther Binding, *Baubetrieb im Mittelalter*, Darmstadt, 1993, 433–44, in an exhaustive treatment of medieval construction, only briefly discussed vaulting or centering; the manuscripts he cites from the early middle ages rarely illustrate formwork for vaults. In a typical example of the French methodology of "archéologie dite des élévations," Jean-Pierre Daugas, ed., *L'Échafaudage dans le chantier médiéval* (Documents d'archéologie en Rhône-Alpes 13), Lyons, 1996, in an excellent survey of scaffolding, did not discuss issues of centering and vaulting.

5. C. Edson Armi, "The Corbel Table," *Gesta* 39/2, 2000, 89–116.

6. Although they often expressed their views deterministically, nineteenth-century writers underscored the importance of practical considerations for understanding the aesthetics of building. See Robert Willis, "On the Construction of the Vaults of the Middle Ages," *Transactions of the Royal Institute of British Architects*, London, 1, 1842, 1–69, at 2: "For the forms and proportions of every structure are so entirely dependent upon its construction and derived from it, that unless we

181

thoroughly understand these constructions, and the methods and reasons which governed and limited them, we shall never succeed in obtaining the master key to their principles"; Eugène Emmanuel Viollet-le-Duc, "Construction," *Dictionnaire raisonné de l'architecture française du XIe au XVIe siècle*, Paris, 10 vols., 1854–68, 4: 1: "L'architecture et la construction doivent être enseignées ou pratiquées simultanément: la construction est le moyen; l'architecture, le résultat." The integrated approach expressed by these men differs from one based on a single or narrow methodology (see Alain Guerreau, "Vingt et une petites églises romanes du Mâconnais: Irrégularités et métrologie," in Patrice Beck, ed., *L'Innovation technique au Moyen Âge: Actes du VIe congrès international d'archéologie médiévale, 1–5 octobre 1996, Dijon*, Paris, 1998, 186–210).

7. For the historiography and theory of Cluniac architecture and sculpture, see C. Edson Armi, *Masons and Sculptors in Romanesque Burgundy: The New Aesthetic of Cluny III*, University Park, Pa., 1983, 24–32. Summarizing the state of research on the pointed arch, Jean Bony, *French Gothic Architecture of the 12th and 13th Centuries*, Berkeley and Los Angeles, 1983, 17, concluded that "the pointed arch made its appearance in a properly Romanesque context at Cluny in southern Burgundy, at an early stage in the construction of the next church, begun by Saint Hugh of Semur in 1088, the church known as Cluny III"; see also Minott Kerr, "The Former Cluniac Priory Church of Paray-le-Monial: A Study of Its Architecture and Sculpture," Ph.D. diss., History of Art Dept., Yale University, 1994, 185–97; and Dietrich Conrad, *Kirchenbau im Mittelalter: Bauplanung und Bauausführung*, Leipzig, 1990. For earlier statements citing the appearance in northern Europe of the pointed arch in the context of Burgundian High Romanesque barrel-vault construction, see Louis Grodecki, *Gothic Architecture*, New York, 1976; Laura Cristiani Testi, "L'arco acuto in Francia nei secoli XI e XII, e le coincidenze con le architetture monastiche in Italia," *Critica d'arte* 11, 1964, 19–30; Kenneth John Conant, *A Brief Commentary on Early Medieval Architecture*, Baltimore, 1942, 30; idem, "Observations on the Vaulting Problems of the Period 1088–1211," *Gazette des beaux-arts* 6/26, 1944, 127–34, at 127; idem, "Early Examples of the Pointed Arch and Vault in Romanesque Architecture," *Viator* 2, 1971, 203–9, at 207; E. Ranquet and H. Ranquet, "Origine française du berceau roman," *Bulletin monumental* 90, 1931, 35–74, at 59; Robert de Lasteyrie, *L'Architecture religieuse en France à l'époque romane*, Paris, 1929, 320–3; Jules Quicherat, *Mélanges d'archéologie et d'histoire: Archéologie du Moyen Âge*, Paris, 1886, 74–85, 147–50. Jean Virey, *Les Églises romanes de l'ancien diocèse de Mâcon: Cluny et sa région*, Mâcon, 1935, 30, was one of the few writers to recognize that the pointed arch occurred in Burgundy from the first part of the eleventh century. He cited the appearance of the point in the context of the barrel vault and identified it in the church at Farges, whose vaults now are dated to the end of the eleventh or beginning of the twelfth century (see Lasteyrie, ibid., 428 n. 1).

8. For discussion of the geometry and construction of the pointed arch in Iran in the eleventh century, see Laleh Haeedah, "Les Arcs brisés persans: Remarques sur leurs particularités géometriques et techniques," *Histoire de l'art* 11, 1990, 3–13.

9. S. Bonde, R. Mark, and E. C. Robison, "Walls and Other Vertical Elements," in Robert Mark, ed., *Architectural Technology up to the Scientific Revolution*, Cambridge, Mass., 1993, 52–137, at 100–22, described change in medieval architecture largely as a sequence of structural problems to be solved. John Fitchen, *The Construction of Gothic Cathedrals: A Study of Medieval Vault Erection*, Chicago, 1961, 40, outlined "the most logical sequence of development for the overall medieval progression, in retrospect." This "sort of ideal stream" of structural development in the Middle Ages progressed from the low and heavy barrel vault to the high and thin-shelled

rib vault. Viollet-le-Duc, *Dictionnaire*, 4: 29–31, described in specifically structural terms the change to the pointed arch in the twelfth century: "The adoption of the pointed arch notably was the result of observations constructors had made about the deformations in round-headed arches." He also related the appearance of the pointed arch to the increasingly secular and scientific attitudes of the twelfth century. Occasionally writers did cite the simultaneous development of the groin and barrel vault. For example, Eugène Lefèvre-Pontalis, *Les Voûtes en berceau et d'arêtes sans doubleaux*, Paris, 1921, in arguing against the early position of the "school" of Auvergne, described the simultaneous existence of groin and barrel vaults with and without transverse arches; see also Heinrich Glück, *Der Ursprung des römischen und abendländischen Wölbungsbaues*, Vienna, 1933, 186–9.

10. Texts and illustrations also do not describe in detail either the men who built early eleventh-century architecture or the circumstances under which they worked. Eliane Vergnolle, "Les Débuts de l'art roman dans le royaume franc (ca. 980–ca. 1020)," *Cahiers de civilisation médiévale* 43/2, 2000, 161–94, at 183–4. Xavier Barral i Altet, "930–1030: L'Aube des temps nouveaux? Histoire et archéologie monumentale," in Barral i Altet, ed., *Le Paysage monumental de la France autour de l'an mil: Colloque international C.N.R.S., Hugues Capet 987–1987: La France de l'an mil, juin–septembre 1987*, Paris, 1987, 9–61, at 38.

11. Armi, "Corbel Table," 93–5.

12. Josep Puig i Cadafalch, "Decorative Forms of the First Romanesque Style," *Art Studies* 4, 1926, 11–99, at 89, 90, 94, 98: "[A]rchitecture was ceasing to be an expression of popular feeling, and was becoming more personal. So it escaped increasingly from the restrictions of rules and regulations; the work of imagination superseded and surpassed that of popular tradition. . . . The first Romanesque style represents the first stage in the formation of a language; the second, the moment when it produces in literature enduring masterpieces, profoundly human."

13. Pierre de Truchis, "L'Architecture lombarde: Ses origines, son extension dans le centre, l'est et le midi de l'Europe," *Congrès archéologique* 76, 1909, 204–42, at 213; Charles Oursel, *L'Art roman de Bourgogne: Études d'histoire et d'archéologie*, Dijon, 1928, 57; Virey, *Les Églises romanes*, xiii.

14. Oursel, *L'Art roman*, 55: "Or nos architectes du XIᵉ siècle demandaient essentiellement l'équilibre à l'entassement des matériaux. . . . Les murs sont donc énormes, les piles volumineuses, les arcs épais et grossiers, les portées assez réduites par un compartimentage multiple, les percements timides par crainte de compromettre la solidité des murailles. L'ensemble est lourd et pesant, et si l'on veut faire grand, on risque aussi de faire plus lourd et plus pesant, d'augmenter les poussées, donc la masse qui les doit contenir. C'est un cercle vicieux." Virey, *Les Églises romanes*, xiii; Armi, *Masons and Sculptors*, 66–7.

15. Oursel, *L'Art roman*, 56: "C'est, en un mot, un art primitif ou primaire, qui ne peut guère, par ses propres moyens, sortir de lui-même. Mais à la fin du XIᵉ siècle, grâce à Cluny, l'architecture bourguignonne va réussir à s'en évader rapidement"; Virey, *Les Églises romanes*, viii. For a critique of "Cluny as the originator as well as diffuser of its architectural type," see Meyer Schapiro, review of Oursel, *L'Art roman*, in *Art Bulletin* 11, 1929, 227–8.

16. The concept of early Burgundian Romanesque architecture as combining superficial Lombard decoration on static, massive volumes continues to be endorsed, especially by writers who believe that these churches were covered inside and out with a coat of plaster. See, for example, discussion under the titles "Une Ambition limitée" and "Un Dilemme: Éclairer ou voûter?" by Eliane Vergnolle, *L'Art roman en France*, Paris, 1994, 73, 96.

CHAPTER ONE: HISTORY, GEOGRAPHY, AND CONSTRUCTION

1. Scholars have remarked that by the twelfth century, Catalan documents use the terms *lombard, lambardus, llambart* to describe stonemasons or masters of the work; see Josep Puig i Cadafalch, *Santa Maria de la Seu d'Urgell*, Barcelona, 1918, 42. Lombard masons may have been referred to as *magistri comacini* because they worked in teams (comasons) or because they came from Lake Como; see Arthur Kingsley Porter, *Lombard Architecture*, New Haven, 1917, 4 vols., 1: 8–20; Josep Puig i Cadafalch, "Les Influences lombardes en Catalogne," *Congrès archéologique de France* 73, 1906, 684–703. On the historiography of this issue, see C. Edson Armi, *Masons and Sculptors in Romanesque Burgundy: The New Aesthetic of Cluny III*, University Park, Pa., 1983, 70 n. 2; and Mathias Delcor, "Joseph Puig i Cadafalch, historien de l'art roman," *Les Cahiers de Saint-Michel-de-Cuxa* 16, 1985, 25–50, at 28. In particular, see Alice L. Sunderland, "The Legend of the Alternate System at Saint-Bénigne of Dijon," *Journal of the Society of Architectural Historians* 12, 1958, 2–9, at 2–3.

On the debate over the impact of William of Volpiano on French architecture, see Neithard Bulst, "Guillaume de Dijon, le bâtisseur de la rotonde," in Monique Jannet and Christian Sapin, eds., *Guillaume de Volpiano et l'architecture des rotondes: Actes de colloque* (Dijon, 23–25 septembre 1993), Dijon, 1996, 19–29, at 19–20. Adriano Peroni, "Le Décor monumental peint et plastique en stuc dans la Lombardie du Xᵉ–XIᵉ siècle (résumé)," *Les Cahiers de Saint-Michel-de-Cuxa* 21, 1990, 109–13, at 110, drew some interesting conclusions from the text (Patr. lat. 142, c. 651) about William of Volpiano. Peroni reconstructed William's travels ("in Italia et in Gallia") as having occurred via the Alps, through northern Italy in the Piedmont and Lombardy. Peroni also retranslated the text ("ac si mundus ipse . . . candidam vestem indueret") as referring to a "splendid" robe of churches in this region, instead of to the "white" robe of churches, usually taken to mean ashlar buildings in northern France. It is also possible that the robe referred to in the text may describe plaster on the exterior of ashlar frame-and-fill churches in northern France. Another important Burgundian figure, Abbot Mayeul of Cluny, in the tenth century is known to have made numerous trips to Italy, including several passes over the Alps (Dominique Iogna-Prat, "Saint Maïeul de Cluny, le provençal entre histoire et légende," in Dominique Iogna-Prat, Barbara H. Rosenwein, Xavier Barral i Altet, and Guy Barruol, *Saint Maïeul, Cluny et la Provence: Expansion d'une abbaye à l'aube du Moyen Âge*, Mane, 1994, 7–14, at 12–13).

For criticism of the concept of *magistri comacini* and the impact of Lombard masons on western Europe, see Eliane Vergnolle, "Les Débuts de l'art roman dans le royaume franc (ca. 980–ca. 1020)," *Cahiers de civilisation médiévale* 43/2, 2000, 161–94, at 179–82; Adriano Peroni, "Arte dell'XI secolo: Il ruolo di Milano e dell'area lombarda nel quadro europeo," *Atti dell'XI Congresso internazionale di studi sull'alto medioevo*, Spoleto, 1989, 751–81; and Marcel Durliat, "La Catalogne et le 'premier art roman,'" *Bulletin monumental* 147/3, 1989, 209–38, at 238, who argued for a more inclusive notion of First Romanesque architecture and its sources: "On méconnait donc certaines orientations essentielles de l'art roman catalan lorsqu'on privilégie les seules relations avec l'Italie." On the convergence of multiple traditions of construction in Burgundy, see Christian Sapin, ed., *Les Prémices de l'art roman en Bourgogne: D'Auxerre à Cluny, les premiers édifices romans après l'an mil*, Auxerre, 1999; idem, "La Pierre et le voûtement: Innovation dans les techniques de construction des églises en Bourgogne au XIᵉ siècle," in Patrice Beck, ed., *L'Inno-*

vation technique au Moyen Âge: Actes du VIᵉ congrès international d'archéologie médiévale, 1–5 octobre 1996, Dijon, Paris, 1998, 179–85, described stone and vaulting construction in Burgundy from 800 to 1200 as a convergence of innovations and building traditions (a position contrasting with my own view that, at the beginning of the eleventh century, masons who built with brick-shaped stones primarily relied upon the Lombard tradition of brick construction); idem, "La Technique de construction en pierre autour de l'an mil, contribution à une réflexion et perspectives de recherches," in Daniel Prigent and Noël-Yves Tonnerre, eds., *La Construction en Anjou au Moyen Âge: Actes de la table ronde d'Angers des 29 et 30 mars 1996.* Angers, 1998, 13–31; idem, "Bourgogne," in Xavier Barral i Altet, ed., *Le Paysage monumental de la France autour de l'an mil: Colloque international C.N.R.S., Hugues Capet 987–1987: La France de l'an mil, juin–septembre 1987,* Paris, 1987, 197–216; Wilhelm Schlink, *Saint-Bénigne in Dijon,* Berlin, 1978, 144 n. 451, described the concept of *magistri comacini* as an art-historical "phantom," arguing: "Die Quellen berichten von italienischen Bautrupps mit keinem Wort." See also Pierre du Colombier, *Les Chantiers des cathédrales: Ouvriers, architectes, sculpteurs,* Paris, 1973, 135; Mario Salmi, "Maestri comacini o commàcini?" *Artigianato e tecnica nella società dell'alto medioevo occidentale: Settimane di Studi di Spoleto XVIII,* Spoleto, 1971, 1: 409–24; 2: 515–16; Claude Poinssot, "Le Bâtiment du dortoir de l'abbaye de Saint-Bénigne de Dijon," *Bulletin monumental* 112, 1954, 303–30, at 317; and Jean Vallery-Radot, "Le Premier Art roman de l'Occident méditerranéen (à propos d'un livre récent)," *La Revue de l'art ancien et moderne* 55, 1929, 105–22, 153–69.

2. Why masons evolved a new building style in Italy and then transmitted their ideas throughout southern Europe, however, remains an open question. Pierre de Truchis, in a groundbreaking article on the origins of Lombard architecture, proposed that a building explosion in the tenth century occurred against a background of cultural changes. He described specifically the fall of the Carolingian dynasty in Italy, the attempt by Ottonian emperors to rekindle Roman political unity, and the renaissance of traditional Early Christian arts and architecture based on prototypes at Ravenna (Pierre de Truchis, "L'Architecture lombarde: Ses origines, son extension dans le centre, l'est et le midi de l'Europe," *Congrès archéologique* 76, 1909, 202–42, at 204–12). Truchis attributed to the abbey of Cluny a strong role in reviving and propagating the Constantinian tradition of severe, brick, arcaded forms. In particular, the Cluniac abbot Odo supported a return to basics, and monks of other orders at Saint-Gall, Reichenau, and Monte Casino shared his enthusiasm for "Gregorian" reform. Pierre Lacroix, *Églises jurassiennes romanes et gothiques: Histoire et architecture,* Besançon, 1981, 9, listed early churches associated with Cluny in the transitional Jura region. See also his discussion (pp. 15–16) of the historiography of medieval architecture in the Franche-Comté. In a historiographic overview, Hans Rudolf Sennhauser, *Romainmôtier und Payerne: Studien zur Cluniazenserarchitektur des 11. Jahrhunderts in der Westschweiz,* Basel, 1970, 35–7, distinguished an earlier phase of scholarship, dependent on Viollet-le-Duc, that argued for the priority of Cluny in creating and transmitting the earliest Romanesque architectural types in eastern France, from a later phase of scholarship that argued for connections between First Romanesque architecture in France and Switzerland based on "regional verbreitete Gemeinsamkeiten."

3. The ethnic makeup of the early settlers, particularly the numbers of Burgundians in the Valley of Aosta, is debated. See Bernard Janin, *Une Région alpine originale: Le Val d'Aoste, tradition et renouveau,* Grenoble, 1968, 123–4, especially n. 36; Walther von Wartburg, *Les Origines des peuples romans,* Paris, 1941; Andrea Zanotto,

Histoire de la Vallée d'Aoste, Aosta, 1968. For the debate over the issue of ethnic fusion in the year 1000, see Christian Lauranson-Rosaz, "La Romanité du Midi de l'an mil," in Robert Delort, ed., *La France de l'an mil,* Paris, 1990, 49–73.

4. Roland Fiétier, ed., *Histoire de la Franche-Comté: Naissance et essor du Comté (XIe–XIIIe siècle),* Toulouse, 1977, 98: "En fait, nulle implantation germanique ne semble avoir suffi à modifier de façon décisive le vieux fonds de population gallo-romaine du pays." On the possibility that the impact of Norman and Hun invasions on the region of eastern France has been overstated, see Yves Jeannin, "Franche-Comté: Orientations de l'archéologie," in Barral i Altet, ed., *Le Paysage monumental,* 327–31, at 327; Bernand Vregille, "Les Origines chrétiennes et le Haut Moyen Âge," in Claude Fohlen, ed., *Histoire de Besançon,* 1964, 231–4.

5. Fiétier, *Franche-Comté,* 114; Émile Magnien, *Histoire de Mâcon et du Mâconnais,* Mâcon, 1971, 50–69; Georges Duby, *La Société aux XIe et XIIe siècles dans la région mâconnaise,* Paris, [1953] 1982; Bernard Bligny, *L'Église et les ordres religieux dans le royaume de Bourgogne aux XIe et XIIe siècles,* Grenoble, 1960, 10–11; René Poupardin, *Le Royaume de Bourgogne (888–1038): Étude sur les origines du royaume d'Arles,* Paris, 1907, 1–3, 211–20; Odet Perrin, *Les Burgondes: Leur histoire, des origines à la fin du premier royaume (534),* Neuchâtel, 1968.

6. René Tournier, "Aspects de l'architecture religieuse en Franche-Comté," *Congrès archéologique* 118, 1960, 9–17, at 12: "Le comté de Bourgogne demeura intégré à l'Empire jusqu'à la convention de Vincennes en 1295."

7. Simone Escoffier, *La Rencontre de la langue d'oïl, de la langue d'oc et du franco-provençal entre Loire et Allier: Limites phonétiques et morphologiques,* Paris, 1958, 172–80, in a detailed study of modern language, outlined the western borders of the Franco-Provençal dialect. She did not locate any early eleventh-century texts that used this dialect (pp. 8–11); Christopher Cope, *Phoenix Frustrated: The Lost Kingdom of Burgundy,* London, 1986, 94–5, 239–46; Georges Straka, ed., *Les Dialectes de France au Moyen Âge et aujourd'hui: Domaines d'oïl et domaine franco-provençal,* Paris, 1972; Pierre Bec, *La Langue occitane,* Paris, 1967, 20–4; Colette Dondaine, *Les Parlers comtois d'oïl: Étude phonétique,* Paris, 1972; Armand Decour, *Le Patois de Bettant: Généralités extraits de la grammaire, curiosités,* Mantes, 1966; Helmut Stimm, *Studien zur Entwicklungsgeschichte des Frankoprovenzalischen,* Wiesbaden, 1952; Albert Dauzat, *La Géographie linguistique,* Paris, 1922; Édouard Bourciez, *Éléments de linguistique romane,* Paris, 1923; Émile Vuarnet, *Patois de Savoie, Dauphiné et Suisse,* Thonon, 1907; G. I. Ascoli, "Schizzi franco-provenzali," *Archivio glottologico italiano* 3, 1878, 61–120.

8. For the Franco-Provençal "dialect boundary controversy" and the historiography of the problem, see George Jochnowitz, *Dialect Boundaries and the Question of Franco-Provençal,* The Hague, 1973, 19–56. The concept of an entity of Franco-Provençal dialect has existed since the end of the nineteenth century. Except for a minority viewpoint that holds that a threefold linguistic division of France is arbitrary (Robert A. Hall Jr., "The Linguistic Position of Franco-Provençal," *Language [Journal of the Linguistic Society of America]* 25, 1949, 1–14, at 14; idem, *External History of the Romance Languages,* New York, 1974, 86), scholars who study the Franco-Provençal issue, if they disagree, do so only about the specific boundaries of the dialect.

9. Pierre Gardette, *Études de géographie linguistique,* Strasbourg, 1983, 607: "Le francoprovençal est une portion curieusement découpée dans le sud-est de la France. Il renferme des morceaux de montagnes et de cours d'eau: morceau des Alpes, morceau du Rhône, quelques plaines à l'est de Lyon, quelques collines.

Beaucoup d'autres régions en France sont mieux délimitées, comme la Gascogne, le Massif Central. . . . Le francoprovençal n'est pas un pays."

10. Janin, *Val d'Aoste*, 55. Even the Grand-Saint-Bernard station, at the peak of the valley, on average has less than two meters of precipitation per year. Precipitation in French Alpine valleys such as the Tarentaise and Maurienne is higher (pp. 56–61).

11. Ibid., 114; Germaine Veyret and Paul Veyret, "Essai de définition de la montagne," *Revue de géographie alpine* 50, 1962, 5–37, at 19–21.

12. For the ancient and medieval road linking the Jura to Italy via the Grand-Saint-Bernard pass, see Yves Renouard, "Les Voies de communication entre la France et le Piémont au Moyen Âge," *Bollettino storico-bibliografico subalpino*, 61, 1963, 233; Pierre Duparc, *Le Comté de Genève IXᵉ–XVᵉ siècle*, Geneva, 1955, 520–65; Fiétier, *Franche-Comté*, 67; Albert Grenier, *Manuel d'archéologie gallo-romaine*, 2ᵉ partie: *Les Routes*, 1934, 23, 36–8, 42. Jacques Thirion, "L'Influence lombarde dans les Alpes françaises du sud," *Bulletin monumental* 128, 1970, 7–40, at 8–9, made a similar point about the Alpine connections between Provence and Lombardy. He showed that the surviving Roman Alpine route from Susa to Apt, following the Valley of the Durance and not the Mediterranean coast, in the Middle Ages was the primary link between Provence and Lombardy. For a cautionary note on the research on Roman roads, see Adrien Blanchet, *L'Archéologie gallo-romaine*, Paris, 1935, 37–9; Jean-Françoise Bergier, "Géographie des cols alpins à la fin du Moyen Âge: Quelques remarques d'ordre méthodologique et chronologique sur le trafic alpin," *Bulletin Annuel de la Fondation Suisse* 4, 1955, 11–27; P. Barocelli, *La strada e le costruzioni romane della Alpis Graia*, Turin, 1924.

13. My translation of Gardette, *Études de géographie linguistique*, 699. Even in the early eleventh century, this region was by no means a cultural monolith. In particular, communes were divided by the investiture controversy, and certain episcopacies, in particular that of Milan under Bishop Aribert of Intimiano, did not hesitate to express a "tendance expansionniste" (Sandro Chierici, *Lombardie romane*, Pierre-qui-vire, 1978, 17). By the thirteenth century, circulation over the Alps through the Valley of Aosta had rapidly declined; see Janin, *Val d'Aoste*, 127–31.

14. By the end of the tenth century, the powerful abbots of Cluny maintained close connections in northern Italy, and frequently traveled there. See the discussion of "une politique italienne" by Iogna-Prat, "Saint Maïeul de Cluny," 12–13. On the pattern of monastic settlement ("colonisation routière") in the western Alps, see Raoul Blanchard, *Les Alpes occidentales*, Grenoble, 7 vols., 1941–56, 3 (1943): 312.

15. For a discussion of the historiography of this consensus, see Guy Fourquin, *Lordship and Feudalism in the Middle Ages*, London, 1976, 65–9; Robert Fossier, *Peasant Life in the Medieval West*, London, 1988, 48–9 (he identified the "new world" transformation as occuring slightly earlier); idem, *La Société médiévale*, Paris, 1991; idem, *Villages et villageois au Moyen Âge*, Paris, 1995, 18; T. N. Bisson, "Forward," in Pierre Bonnassie, *From Slavery to Feudalism in Southwestern Europe*, Cambridge, 1991, ix–xi; Guy Bois, *The Transformation of the Year One Thousand: The Village of Lournand from Antiquity to Feudalism*, Manchester, 1992, 7, 25, 98.

16. Edmond Pognon, *La Vie quotidienne en l'an mil*, Paris, 1981, 23.

17. Robert Fossier, *Enfance de l'Europe Xᵉ–XIIᵉ siècle: Aspects économiques et sociaux*, Paris, 2 vols., 1982, 1: 99; Fossier, *Peasant Life*, 8–9.

18. Duby, *La Société*, 33.

19. Georges Duby, *Guerriers et paysans, VIIᵉ–XIIᵉ siècle: Premier essor de l'économie*

européenne, Paris, 1973, 162; Bonnassie, *La Catalogne au tournant de l'an mil: Croissance et mutations d'une société*, Paris, 1990, 35, 56–7.

20. Robert S. Lopez, *The Birth of Europe*, New York, 1966, 112–14.

21. Bois, *Transformation*, 65; Bonnassie, *From Slavery to Feudalism*, 109, 119; idem, *La Catalogne*, 292–4; Fossier, *Peasant Life*, 126–9; Duby, *La Société*, 137–45; Joaquim Nadal Farreras and Philippe Wolff, ed., *Histoire de la Catalogne*, Toulouse, 1982, 245–8; Jean-Pierre Poly, *La Provence et la société féodale (879–1166)*, Paris, 1976, 29, 100–13, 130.

22. On the "gift and counter-gift" relationship between local lords and monasteries, see Georges Duby, *Art and Society in the Middle Ages*, Cambridge, 2000, 28–9.

23. Pierre Riché, *Écoles et enseignement dans le haut Moyen Âge, fin du Ve siècle–milieu du XIe siècle*, Paris, 1989, 140–1.

24. Bonnassie, *La Catalogne*, 244; Xavier Barral i Altet, "930–1030: L'Aube des temps nouveaux? Histoire et archéologie monumentale," in Barral i Altet, ed., *Le Paysage monumental*, 9–61, at 45.

25. Bois, *Transformation*, 41, 136, 153–4; Duby, *La Société*, 139–41.

26. Jerrilynn D. Dodds, *Architecture and Ideology in Early Medieval Spain*, University Park, Pa., 1990, 113.

27. Odillo was an abbot statesman who energetically traveled across Europe and maintained important connections with the King of Navarre, Stephen of Hungary, Casimir I of Poland, and even the Emperor Henry II; see Eleanor Duckett, *Death and Life in the Tenth Century*, Ann Arbor, 1967, 210. Similarly, many letters, sermons, and poems of Oliba reveal his international perspective and show him to have incorporated the literature and viewpoints of many cultures, past and present, into his thoughts; see Henri Focillon, *The Year 1000*, New York, 1969, 85; Riché, *Écoles*, 159–61. Bonnassie, *La Catalogne*, 254–5, described the manuscripts at Vic, where Oliba had been bishop, as a "veritable anthology of all the pagan and Christian classics."

28. Georges Duby, *Féodalité*, Paris, 1996, 139–41.

29. André Chédeville, Jacques Le Goff, and Jacques Rossiaud, *La Ville en France au Moyen Âge*, Paris, 1998.

30. Poly, *La Provence*, 12–13.

31. Pognon, *La Vie quotidienne*, 57–8.

32. Duby, *La Société*, 138–45; Farreras and Wolff, *Histoire de la Catalogne*, 251–3; Ramon d'Abadal i de Vinyals et al., *Moments crucials de la història de Catalunya*, Barcelona, 1962, 42–3; d'Abadal, *Els primers comtes catalans*, Barcelona, 1958.

33. Duby, *Féodalité*, 151: "[L]'expulsion des Sarrasins permit de restaurer les monastères qui servaient de relais au long des itinéraires de montagne, c'est-à-dire aux alentours de l'An Mil, des relations que le brigandage n'avait jamais interrompues s'intensifièrent entre les carrefours lombards et les pays d'au-delà des Alpes."

34. Duby, *Féodalité*, 143; Fossier, *Société médiévale*, 260.

35. Bois, *Transformation*, 48, 165; Duby, *La Société*, 51, 277–8.

36. Bonnassie, *From Slavery to Feudalism*, 108; idem, *La Catalogne*, 182–8; Farreras and Wolff, *Histoire de la Catalogne*, 254 .

37. Fossier, *Enfance de l'Europe*, 1: 1044–61.

38. Duby, *La Société*, 279; Bonnassie, *La Catalogne*, 246, suggested that in Catalonia in the early eleventh century, increased commercial exchange encouraged the rise of architectural specialists (*magistri edorum*), who traveled to different sites and were paid for their expertise: "La précoce naissance de l'art roman catalan doit donc être considérée, sans hésitation, comme l'un des fruits de la croissance économique du pays."

39. That is not to say that, within the transalpine region, masons did not express distinct local architectural preferences, such as those described by S. Chierici, *Lombardie romane*, 24–5; Raymond Oursel, *Art en Savoie*, Paris, 1975; Oleg Zastrow, *L'arte romanica del comasco*, Como, 1972; Mariaclotilde Magni, "Sopravvivenze carolinge e ottoniane nell'architettura romanica dell'arco alpino centrale," *Arte lombarda* 14/1, 1969, 35–44; 14/2, 1969, 77–87; Anna Finocchi, *L'architettura romanica nel territorio di Varese*, Milan, 1966; Edoardo Arslan, "L'architettura romanica milanese," in *Storia di Milano*, 1954, 3: 397–521.

40. Arthur Kingsley Porter, *The Construction of Lombard and Gothic Vaults*, New Haven, 1911, 19: "Throughout the vast triangle the sides of which are determined by the Alps, the Apennines, and the Adriatic, brick was the building material which the builders found themselves forced to use. This vast alluvial region is practically without stone, while clays for terra cottas and bricks abound. Wood is scarce." For a different point of view on the availability of wood in this region, see S. Chierici, *Lombardie romane*, 25–6.

41. On the difference between solid-brick Early Christian construction in Milan and brick-faced concrete Early Christian construction in Rome, see Richard Krautheimer, *Early Christian and Byzantine Architecture*, Baltimore, 1986, 78–92.

42. Paolo Verzone, *L'architettura romanica del novarese*, Novara, 2 vols., 1935–6.

43. Armi, *Masons and Sculptors*, 43, 121–5. For analysis and discussion of the historiography of this tradition of frame-and-fill construction in northern France, see Daniel Prigent and Jean-Yves Hunot, "Les Édifices religieux antérieurs à l'an mil en Anjou," in Daniel Prigent and Noël-Yves Tonnerre, eds., *La Construction en Anjou au Moyen Âge: Actes de la table ronde d'Angers des 29 et 30 mars 1996*, Angers, 1998, 33–54.

44. Josep Puig i Cadafalch, *La Géographie et les origines du premier art roman*, Paris, 1935, 101, understood the impact of the tradition of brick building on the techniques of stone construction. He maintained that "l'architecture lombarde en pierre est une traduction de formes antiques créées d'abord pour la brique, pour un rectangle allongé. C'est la géologie du pays d'origine qui lui impose ses formes constructives." In contrast, the area of the Bresse, between the Jura and the Mâconnais, was not favored with good building stone, and masons who practiced brick-construction techniques rarely built churches in this region. See Raymond Oursel, "Tableau de la Bresse romane," in René Tournier, ed., *Franche-Comté romane*, Pierre-qui-vire, 1979, 273–86, at 282: "Il faut renoncer donc à rechercher en Bresse un maillon quelconque de la chaîne qui, par-dessus son espace, unit les monuments de Comté et de Bourgogne méridionale authentiquement et chronologiquement affectés par ce style très dru, et l'intermédiaire recherché entre les églises de Saint-Hymetière d'une part, de Tournus et de Combertault de l'autre, liées par les affinités structurales que l'on sait."

45. Jean-François Garmier, *Le Guide du Mâconnais*, Paris, 1990, 19, 110: "Le calcaire mâconnais se présente dans les carrières en lits peu épais, ce qui explique la minceur des moellons." See Jean Vallery-Radot, *Saint-Philibert de Tournus*, 1955, 204.

46. Related to this masonry technique is the earlier Mâconnais construction based on large *opus spicatum*. This building technique can be seen in the churches of Saint-Mayeul and Cluny II at Cluny, and in churches at Bonnay and Saint Clément-sur-Guye. For a discussion of the *opus spicatum* in these buildings, see Armi, *Masons and Sculptors*, 129 n. 23.

47. Most of the ashlar decoration in the upper narthex and cloister of Saint-Philibert at Tournus was not designed for its current location. See C. Edson Armi,

"The Nave of Saint-Philibert at Tournus," *Journal of the Society of Architectural Historians* 60/1, 2001, 46–67, at 60–4; idem, *Masons and Sculptors,* 139–40.

48. For a recent overview of the bibliography and historiography of Saint-Philibert at Tournus, see Jacques Henriet, *Saint-Philibert de Tournus, l'abbatiale du XIᵉ siècle*, Paris, 1992; Sebastian Helm et al., *Saint-Philibert in Tournus: Baugeschichte und architekturgeschichtliche Stellung*, Freiburg, 1988. On the use of brick techniques in the Tournus narthex, see C. Edson Armi, "The Corbel Table," *Gesta* 39/2, 2000, 89–116, at 89–92, 102–4.

49. Even where masons exceptionally used ashlar blocks, as on the exterior of the facade, they laid them as bricks that course through vertical bands. Used in this way, the ashlar courses stabilize the wall at the level that the lateral barrels meet the facade.

CHAPTER TWO: THE POINTED ARCH AND GROIN VAULT IN NORTHERN ITALY

1. Arthur Kingsley Porter, *Lombard Architecture*, New Haven, 1917, 4 vols., 2: 502, 507, proposed that after the counts palatine of Pavia had been driven from that city, they established themselves at Lomello about the year 1018, built or rebuilt the castle, and reconstructed the village church. He determined that masons about the turn of the thirteenth century in "great part" reconstructed the side aisle vaults, although in the ruined western bays they left traces of the original vaults in the north aisle. In the eighteenth century, restorers installed a new facade that left the western bays of the nave open to the elements; idem, "Santa Maria Maggiore di Lomello," *Arte e Storia*, 30, 1911, 175–81. See also Gian Franco Magenta, *Le chiese di Lomello*, Vigevano, 1999; Adriano Peroni, "Arte dell'XI secolo: Il ruolo di Milano e dell'area lombarda nel quadro europeo," *Atti dell'XI Congresso internazionale di studi sull'alto medioevo*, Spoleto, 1989, 751–81, at 755–8; Gino Chierici, "La chiesa di S. Maria Maggiore a Lomello," *Palladio* 1, 1951, 67–93; Sandro Chierici, *Lombardie romane*, Pierre-qui-vire, 1978, 307–13. According to Gino Chierici, "La chiesa," 67–9, the crypt was begun before the present church but never finished. Hans Thümmler, "Die Baukunst des 11. Jahrhunderts in Italien," *Römisches Jahrbuch für Kunstgeschichte* 3, 1939, 141–226, at 157–61, without going into details of construction, carefully analyzed the relation of the piers, orders, responds, and vaults at Lomello.

2. These round-headed arches may have functioned as do certain ribs in a Gothic vault. In both cases, masons could have braced the wooden centering, used to build the webs, against the sides of the stone voussoirs; see John Fitchen, *The Construction of Gothic Cathedrals: A Study of Medieval Vault Erection*, Chicago, 1961, 57–62.

3. Gino Chierici, *La chiesa di S. Satiro a Milano e alcune considerazioni sull'architettura preromanica in Lombardia*, Milan, 1942, 65–7, fig. 17, described and illustrated the vaults of the crypt of Sant'Eusebio, Pavia. He showed them to be corbeled on the bottom and radially vaulted on the top. He proposed Early Christian prototypes, such as the central cupola of the baptistry at Fréjus, for the corbeled "false vault." The date of this crypt is disputed; see Adriano Peroni, "La cripta di Sant'-Eusebio: Problemi e prospettive di un restauro in corso," *Pavia*, May–June 1968, 1–26, at 2–3; Porter, *Lombard Architecture*, 3: 167–70.

The horizontally coursed corbel vault had a long history in Europe, even before the Roman period; see Piero Sanpaolesi, "Strutture a cupola autoportanti," *Palladio* 21, 1971, 3–64. Auguste Choisy, *L'Art de bâtir chez les Romains*, Paris, 1873, 35–8, pls. 18, 19, and Giovanni Teresio Rivoira, *Roman Architecture*, trans. G. McN. Rush-forth, London, 1925, 163–5, described the corbeled lower portion of the groin vaults in the Palatine Palace of Septimus Severus. In brick construction, Roman masons corbeled the top of piers in conjunction with "ribbed" groin voussoirs (idem, *Lombardic Architecture, Its Origin, Development and Derivatives*, trans G. McN. Rushforth, London, 1910, 80; Friedrich Wilhelm Deichmann, *Studien zur Architektur Konstantinopels*, Mainz, 1954, 33–4). The primary function of brick ribbing may have been to simplify the process of construction. Masons could have used the ribs to rest the formwork to lay the aggregate (*caementa*) in roughly horizontal courses (John B. Ward-Perkins, *Roman Imperial Architecture*, Harmondsworth, 1981, 98; and William Lloyd MacDonald, *The Architecture of the Roman Empire*, New Haven, 1982, 159).

This technique of corbel-vault construction differs from that frequently found in the groins of Byzantine prototypes. In a Byzantine groin vault, masons typically laid slightly pitched bricks across the axis of the vault, parallel to the extrados of the arches; they relied upon gravity and the adhesion of mortar to keep the bricks in place. These brick courses meet not only in the center but also at the corners of the space to be covered. In other words, in the standard Byzantine vault, masons folded the bricks down into the point of the groin, whereas in the corbel vaults of Italy and Burgundy, masons used the horizontally coursed corners of the webs as cantilevered bases from which they radiated the stones of a true groin vault. On the construction of Byzantine vaults, see Cyril Mango, *Byzantine Architecture*, New York, 1976, pls. 10–13; Richard Krautheimer, *Early Christian and Byzantine Architecture*, Baltimore, 1986, 226, fig. 183; Norman Davey, A *History of Building Materials*, London, 1961, 142–3; Paul Lemerle, *Philippes et la Macédoine orientale à l'époque chrétienne et byzantine: Recherches d'histoire et d'archéologie*, Paris, 1945, 457–60. Earlier authors such as Auguste Choisy, *L'Art de bâtir chez les Byzantins*, Paris, 1883, 49–57, similarly described this kind of Byzantine groin vault. Arthur Kingsley Porter, *The Construction of Lombard and Gothic Vaults*, New Haven, 1911, 6, believed that this type of Byzantine vault influenced creation of the domical Lombard groin vault.

In describing Gothic architecture, John H. Acland, *Medieval Structure: The Gothic Vault*, Toronto, 1972, 82, observed corbeled construction in rib vaults; and Marcel Aubert, "Les Plus Anciennes Croisées d'ogives: Leur rôle dans la construction," *Bulletin monumental* 93, 1934, 5–67, 137–237, at 10, noted that the lower courses of webs often course with ribs in Lombard rib construction.

4. In the southwest tower of San Lorenzo at Milan, masons similarly coursed some of the stones from the corbeled web into the stones of the *formeret* next to the vault; for illustrations, see Roberto Cecchi, "San Lorenzo Maggiore tra XI e XII secolo: Alcuni aspetti costruttivi," in Carlo Bertelli, ed., *Il millennio ambrosiano: La città del vescovo dai Carolingi al Barbarossa*, Milan, 1988, 176–95, at 184. Adriano Peroni, "La struttura del S. Giovanni in Borgo di Pavia e il problema della copertura nell'architettura romanica lombarda," *Arte lombarda* 14/1, 1969, 21–34; 14/2, 1969, 63–76.

5. John Fleming, Hugh Honour, and Nikolaus Pevsner, *The Penguin Dictionary of Architecture*, Baltimore, 1966, 220.

6. The *tas-de-charge* usually is seen as having been developed in the context of the rib and not of the groin vault; see Dieter Kimpel and Robert Suckale, *Die gotische Architektur in Frankreich 1130–1270*, Munich, 1985, 40–1; Fitchen, *Construction*, 75 (see also his bibliography, 218 n. 131); Robert Branner, *Burgundian Gothic Archi-*

tecture, London, 1960, 43; Jean-Auguste Brutails, *Précis d'archéologie du Moyen Âge*, Toulouse, 1936, 300; Eugène Emmanuel Viollet-le-Duc, "Construction," *Dictionnaire raisonné de l'architecture française du XIe au XVIe siècle*, Paris, 10 vols., 1854–68, 4: 93, 168. I do not mean to imply that the principle of the *tas-de-charge* was not in use before the eleventh century.

7. In the course of construction, the springing of a true vault becomes heavily loaded, requiring a stable structure beneath it (Fitchen, *Construction*, 14). In decentering (removal of the formwork after construction), the pressure at the haunches of a true vault also produces a key form of instability and collapse. The risk in both cases is reduced if a corbel vault is used at the base of the vault. The horizontally coursed stones in this kind of vault exert less lateral pressure than the radially laid ones in a true vault. See E. Ranquet and H. Ranquet, "Origine française du berceau roman," *Bulletin monumental* 90, 1931, 35–74, at 40, 45.

8. Auguste Choisy, *Histoire de l'architecture*, Paris, 2 vols., 1929, 2: 98, recognized the advantages of this form of vault construction in Sassanian architecture. Photographs of the restoration of the crypt at Spiez show that by first corbeling the bottom courses of the groin, masons could save on the amount of wooden scaffolding needed to build a true vault. Restorers used the surviving corbeled horizontal courses on the bottom of this vault as a base to spring the real webs of the vault (Walter Sulser, with Alfred Heubach, "Die Restaurierung der Romanischen Kirche von Spiez," *Zeitschrift für schweizerische Archaeologie und Kunstgeschichte* 11/3, 1950, 1–18, at fig. 56). Paolo Verzone, "L'origine della volta lombarda a nervature," *Atti del IV Convegno nazionale di storia dell'architettura, Milano, 18–25 giugno 1939*, 1941, 53–64, did not discuss this constructive purpose; see also Cecchi, "San Lorenzo Maggiore," 187.

9. By associating the corbel system of the *tas-de-charge* with the rib vault, scholars have slighted the groin vault and distorted the very nature of its construction. This slight to the groin, however, does not seem to have been intentional, because authorities on French Romanesque architecture have generally distinguished the construction of true groin vaults from what they considered to be inferior corbeled construction. For example, Robert de Lasteyrie, *L'Architecture religieuse en France à l'époque romane*, Paris, 1929, 322, following Viollet-le-Duc, *Dictionnaire*, 6: 421, in differentiating the construction of these two vault types: "[I]l y a une différence capitale, car à Mycènes les pierres dont l'assemblage dessine un arc brisé sont posées à plat les unes sur les autres, elles forment un simple encorbellement; tandis que dans les voûtes et les arcs brisés de l'époque romane, elles sont toujours posées normalement à la courbe. Pour qui ne considère que l'apparence extérieure des choses, ce détail semble avoir peu d'importance, mais pour le praticien, pour l'archéologue soucieux de pénétrer les principes qui ont présidé au développement de l'art de construire, il en a une grande et c'est ce que Viollet-le-Duc a parfaitement montré."

More recently, scholars have perpetuated this distinction by emphasizing the purely vaulted character of the groin while disregarding its corbeled construction. For example, Robert Mark modeled the "typical construction and surcharge" of a groin vault by extending the true-vault web almost to a point at its base. He pictured the wall behind the base of the web as a dead load that was added separately behind the haunches of the vault, and not coursed to it; Robert Mark, *Experiments in Gothic Structure*, Cambridge, Mass., 1982, 107, fig. 67, and R. Mark and E. C. Robison, "Vaults and Domes," in Robert Mark, *Architectural Technology up to the Scientific Revolution*, Cambridge, Mass., 1993, 138–81, at 163, fig. 4.24; see also Paul Amédée, ed., *Encyclopédie de l'architecture et de la construction*, Paris, 1888, 1: 247.

In the transalpine region, First Romanesque masons usually constructed and supported groin vaults very differently from the way shown in the typical example cited by Mark. In the lower portion of the vault, masons did not separate the vault from the surcharge, but rather continued beds from the webs directly into the corbeled construction of the wall. In this way, they eliminated true-vault construction from the lower portions of the groin and sizably reduced the stress concentration from radiating voussoirs on the small point of springing.

10. Mario Salvadori and Matthys Levy, *Structural Design in Architecture*, Englewood Cliffs, N.J., 1967, 269–73; Mario Salvadori and Robert Heller, *Structure in Architecture: The Building of Buildings*, Englewood Cliffs, N.J., 1963, 296.

11. On the insertion of rubble courses between ribs and vault webbing, see Robert Willis, "On the Construction of the Vaults of the Middle Ages," *Transactions of the Royal Institute of British Architects, London*, 1, 1842, 1–69.

12. Porter, *Lombard Architecture*, 1: 109, 110, and idem, *Construction*, 18, described the appearance of "dying" or "disappearing" webs in groin vaults. The visual effect of webs overlapping the base of arches he attributed to the constructional needs of masons, who built these webs without relying upon transverse and wall arches.

This conclusion is accurate as far as it goes, but it does not take into account the objectives of masons in building the top of the arch. In order to point the web, masons often inserted filler stones that heighten the arch and exaggerate the "dying" effect on the bottom. The statement that the nonconcentric extrados and intrados at the top of the arches in the nave arcade at Lomello serve a "purely ornamental" purpose overlooks the role of these long central voussoirs in the aisle, on the other side of the nave wall. In this location they support the pointed section of the groin webs (see Fig. 15).

13. Viollet-le-Duc, *Dictionnaire*, 4: 36–7, and Francis Bond, *An Introduction to English Church Architecture*, London, 1913, 290, discussed the pointed arch in the context of Gothic architecture. They described the structural advantages for vaulting achieved by substituting pointed transverse arches for semicircular ones.

14. Fitchen, *Construction*, 65.

15. C. Edson Armi, "Orders and Continuous Orders in Romanesque Architecture," *Journal of the Society of Architectural Historians* 34, 1975, 178–88.

16. Before the eleventh century, even in buildings erected with techniques not based on brick, masons had used principles of vaulting that later became common in Lombardy. For example, in the "second campaign" of the ninth-century northern Burgundian crypt at Flavigny, masons employed frame-and-fill construction. They corbeled the lower portion of groin vaults and inserted horizontal filler stones beneath small pointed webs. On the dates of construction at Flavigny, see Christian Sapin, *La Bourgogne préromane: Construction, décor et fonction des édifices religieux*, Paris, 1986, 81–112.

17. I would like to thank the anonymous reviewer from Cambridge University Press, who pointed out that the trajectory of the web rises beyond a semicircle in a few of the vaults against the east and west walls of the crypt at Hersfeld.

18. Scholars have disputed the dates of the crypt of the cathedral at Aosta, although most agree that the eastern three bays preceded the western two. See Daria de Bernardi Ferrero, "Aoste, la cathédrale de Sainte-Marie," *Congrès archéologique* 129, 1978, 157–72; Mariaclotilde Magni, *Architettura religiosa e scultura romanica*

nella Valle d'Aosta, Aosta, 1974, 79–81; idem, "Un Remarquable Témoignage du premier art roman en Italie du nord: La Cathédrale d'Aoste," *Cahiers archéologiques* 24, 1975, 163–72; Sandro Chierici, *Piémont-Ligurie roman,* Pierre-qui-vire, 1979, 203–7; Umberto Chierici, "Fra cultura padana e cultura francese," in Giovanni Agnelli, ed., *Piemonte, Valle d'Aosta,* Milan, 1968, 352–3; Edoardo Arslan, "L'architettura romanica milanese," *Storia di Milano,* Milan, 1954, 3: 397–521, at 423; Porter, *Lombard Architecture,* 1916, 2: 51; Rivoira, *Lombardic Architecture,* 303.

19. The ruined crypt of Sant'Eufemia on the Isola Comacina provides one of the best examples of corbel vaults built with stones in a brick technique. The exposed cross section of these vaults reveals that between adjacent webs the lower courses run horizontally behind the transverse arches. At approximately a quarter of the height of the vault, these courses abruptly stop and form a distinct horizontal suture. In the true vault above this level, masons introduced radially laid stones. For bibliography and illustrations, see S. Chierici, *Lombardie romane,* 38–9; Mariaclotilde Magni, *Architettura romanica comasca,* Milan, 1960, 43–7, figs. 36–37.

20. S. Chierici, *Piémont-Ligurie roman,* 195–202; Raul Capra, *La basilica di S. Michele in Oleggio,* Novara, 1968, fig. X/1,2.

21. Similarly, curves of similarly steeped pitch sometimes can be seen in the sides of round-headed arches without vaults, as in the apse arcade in Saint-Leger at Aymaville, near Aosta. See Magni, *Valle d'Aosta,* 75, Fig. 81. In the crypt of Saint-Dalmas at Valdeblore, Jacques Thirion, "Remarques sur la crypte et les structures récemment dégagées de l'église de Saint-Dalmas-Valdeblore," *Cahiers archéologiques* 38, 1990, 63–79, at 73, observed "les arêtes sinueuses et aplaties à la clef," but he attributed this shape to "malhabile" construction techniques. See also idem, "L'Église Saint-Dalmas de Valdeblore." *Bulletin monumental* 111, 1953, 157–71.

22. Jean Vallery-Radot, "L'Église Saint-Martin à Aime," *Congrès archéologique* 123, 1965, 121–36.

23. Rivoira, *Lombardic Architecture,* 1: 163, 183–5. Unusual vaulting solutions occur with great frequency in Italy because of the number of crypts with irregular bay shapes. See Marcel Durliat, "Problèmes posés par l'histoire de l'architecture religieuse en Catalogne dans la première moitié du XIᵉ siècle," *Les Cahiers de Saint-Michel-de-Cuxa* 3, 1972, 43–9, at 45: "Si la vogue des grandes cryptes est générale en Europe au XIᵉ siècle, elle apparaît singulièrement vive et précoce en Italie"; Jean Hubert, "La Crypte de Saint-Jean-de-Maurienne et l'expansion de l'art lombard en France," *Bulletin de la Société Nationale des Antiquaires de France,* 1961, 40–9; and Jacques Thirion, "L'Influence lombarde dans les Alpes françaises du Sud," *Bulletin monumental* 128, 1970, 7–40.

24. In highly irregular groin vaults, such as in the asymmetrical entry bay on the north side of the crypt at Saint-Leger, Aymaville, Italian masons pointed the stone webs. To do so they used the brick system, seen at Lomello, of inserting filler stones between the round-headed transverse arches and the vault. For an illustration, see Magni, *Valle d'Aosta,* fig. 83.

25. Fitchen, *Construction,* 59: "[S]mall units of this [groin] vaulting erected at relatively low levels, such as those over the bays of the side aisles . . . were doubtless formed on mounded earth." In small-scale vaults, such as those over the corners of tower stairs, masons frequently avoided the step of corbel construction. Instead, they built true vaults from the very base of groin webs. This shortcut can be deduced from the traces of lag boards left in mortal in examples like the crypt at Saint-Jean-de-Maurienne. See Anna Segagni Malacart, "La 'Torre Civica' di Pavia

e le torri campanarie padane del secolo XI," *Arte medievale* 4/2, 1990, 99–121, at 116; Mariaclotilde Magni, "Le torri campanarie romaniche nel Canton Ticino," *Commentari* 17, 1966, 28–43.

Traces left by a wide trowel on a layer of mortar suggest that masons may have straightened and sharpened the irregular groin lines created by the rough fill in webs. Examples can be seen in groin vaults that have not been replastered, such as in the lower narthex of San Vincenzo at Pombia.

26. Fitchen, *Construction*, 120–1, suggested a similar system in rib vaults for resting centering below the surface of the webs; see also Acland, *Medieval Structure*, 82–3; Jean Vallery-Radot, "Saint-Jean-de-Maurienne, la cathédrale Saint-Jean-Baptiste," *Congrès archéologique* 123, 1965, 49–85.

27. Another option would have been wicker centering. See Malcolm Thurlby, "Observations on Romanesque and Gothic Vault Construction," *Arris* 6, 1995, 22–9.

28. For example, Fleming et al., *Penguin Dictionary of Architecture*, 232, described a groin vault as being "produced" by the "intersection at right angles of two tunnel vaults of identical shape." This typological definition has a long history; see, e.g., Lasteyrie, *L'Architecture religieuse*, 251; Bond, *English Church Architecture*, 286; Russell Sturgis, *A Dictionary of Architecture and Building*, New York, 3 vols., 1902, 3: 326; Choisy, *Byzantins*, 49. Porter, *Construction*, 17–18, 26, provided a notable exception to this kind of definition.

CHAPTER THREE: THE POINTED ARCH AND GROIN VAULT AT THE BEGINNING OF THE ELEVENTH CENTURY IN BURGUNDY

1. C. Edson Armi, "Saint-Philibert at Tournus and Wall Systems of First Romanesque Architecture," Ph.D. diss., Dept. of Art History and Archaeology, Columbia University, 1973, 57–73.

2. For the range of dates given to Saint-Philibert at Tournus, see C. Edson Armi, *Masons and Sculptors in Romanesque Burgundy: The New Aesthetic of Cluny III*, University Park, Pa., 1983, 145–50; for building campaigns, see ibid., 131–44.

3. See John Fitchen, *The Construction of Gothic Cathedrals: A Study of Medieval Vault Erection*, Chicago, 1961, 65, for a discussion of thin-shell theory. He described the creases and curvature in thin groin vaults as a source of stiffness.

4. Pierre de Truchis, "L'Architecture lombarde: Ses origines, son extension dans le centre, l'est et le midi de l'Europe," *Congrès archéologique* 76, 1909, 204–42, at 216, maintained that "cette disposition des voûtes, originaire de l'école romaine d'Orient, avait été appliquée à Rome dans les thermes de Dioclétien."

5. Ernst Gall, "Die Abteikirche Saint-Philibert in Tournus, eine kritische Untersuchung zur frühburgundischen Baukunst," *Der Cicerone* 4, 1912, 624–36, at 626; idem, "St. Philibert in Tournus," *Zeitschrift für Kunstgeschichte* 15, 1952, 179–82, at 182; and Sebastian Helm et al., *Saint-Philibert in Tournus: Baugeschichte und architekturgeschichtliche Stellung*, Freiburg, 1988, 27, argued that, in the lower-story narthex, because the arches supporting the intersection of the transverse barrel vaults spring from points lower than the neckings of the adjacent piers, the transverse barrels must have been added after the piers. This argument is consistent in itself, but it does not correspond with the facts of construction. The horizontal voussoirs at the base of the low arches course with the stones on the adjacent freestanding and attached piers (see Fig. 14); moreover, the stones throughout these piers have an

identical manufacture, showing none of the differences visible in the stones in the piers of the nave and upper narthex. It is highly probable, therefore, that masons at the same time built the arches and piers of the lower narthex.

6. Josep Puig i Cadafalch, *Le Premier Art roman*, Paris, 1928, 136, entertained none of these considerations in describing the "causes" for the use of the groin vault in the lower narthex at Tournus. He pointed to the "ordre géographique, le climat et les matériaux." For his theory on the role of geographic location, climate and material in determining vault selection, see Josep Puig i Cadafalch, *La Géographie et les origines du premier art roman*, Paris, 1935, 138–40.

7. Where adjacent barrel vaults did not exist – for example, beneath the groin vaults in the crypt of Sainte-Marie at Levens – masons did not have to place the transverse arch at a low height (see Fig. 51). They could construct transverse arches with a raised center, a "forme lunulaire," as described by Jacques Thirion, "Un Témoin du premier art roman en Provence: La Madone de Levens," *Bulletin monumental* 119, 1961, 345–51, at 348.

8. On the simultaneous use of groin and barrel vaults in the Carolingian crypt of Saint-Germain at Auxerre, see Christian Sapin, "La Pierre et le voûtement: Innovation dans les techniques de construction des églises en Bourgogne au XIe siècle," in Patrice Beck, ed., *L'Innovation technique au Moyen Âge: Actes du VIe congrès international d'archéologie médiévale, 1–5 octobre 1996, Dijon*, Paris, 1998, 179–85, at 180.

9. Charles Oursel, *L'Art roman de Bourgogne: Études d'histoire et d'archéologie*, Dijon, 1928, 44, understood that "l'architecture romane primitive a employé à peu près toutes les méthodes et toutes les combinaisons de voûtes," but he did not allow that Italian architecture played an important role in the development of Burgundian vaulting types (pp. 51–6).

10. Dendrochronology has been used to date the tower of Saint-Martin at Chapaize; see Christian Sapin, "Dendrochronologie et architecture monumentale dans le haut Moyen Âge; problèmes spécifiques," in Georges Lambert, ed., *Les Veines du temps: Lectures de bois en Bourgogne*, Autun, 1992, 159–75; Danielle Ruset, *Monographie de l'église de Chapaize*, Mâcon, 1983; Jean Virey, "L'Église de Chapaize," *Annales de l'Académie de Mâcon* 27, 1930–1, 437–44.

11. The vaults at Chapaize are now covered by plaster. On the debate over the existence of plaster in early eleventh-century, brick-based churches in southern Burgundy, see C. Edson Armi, "Report on the Destruction of Romanesque Architecture in Burgundy," *Journal of the Society of Architectural Historians* 55/3, 1996, 300–27.

12. Other examples of this kind of necking can be found in the church at Mellecey and the stables of Saint Hugh at Cluny.

13. For bibliography and a discussion of the reconstruction of the *dortoir* of Saint-Bénigne at Dijon, see Wilhelm Schlink, *Saint-Bénigne in Dijon*, Berlin, 1978, 70–6.

14. Armi, "Saint-Philibert at Tournus," 57–73.

15. For other possible early eleventh-century groin-vaulted naves, see F. Galtier Marti, "L'Église ligurienne San Paragorio de Noli et ses rapports avec Santa Maria de Obarra (Aragon) et San Vicente de Cardona (Catalogne): Trois précoces témoignages artistiques de la 'diaspora' lombarde," *Cahiers de Saint-Michel-de-Cuxa* 19, 1988, 151–68. Marcel Durliat, "La Catalogne et le 'premier art roman,'" *Bulletin monumental* 147/3, 1989, 209–38, at 255, argued in the traditional, and more convincing, way that from the start masons intended a barrel vault at Cardona.

CHAPTER FOUR: THE POINTED ARCH AND GROIN VAULT IN BURGUNDY AT THE END OF THE ELEVENTH CENTURY

1. C. Edson Armi, "The Corbel Table," *Gesta* 39/2, 2000, 89–116, at 104–8.

2. C. Edson Armi, *Masons and Sculptors in Romanesque Burgundy: The New Aesthetic of Cluny III*, University Park, Pa., 1983, 53–7.

3. Jean Virey, *Les Églises romanes de l'ancien diocèse de Mâcon: Cluny et sa région*, Mâcon, 1935, 284–94; Charles Dard, *Farges-les-Mâcon*, Mâcon, 1927.

4. See similar examples of broken barrel vaults in Saint-Pierre at Uchizy, and in churches like those at Châteauneuf, Saint-Bonnet-de-Cray, and Semur-en-Brionnais that are related to the narthex of Saint-Fortunat at Charlieu.

5. Beginning in 1970, the Association de Sauvegarde et mise en valeur du Prieuré du Puley restored and reconstructed the vaults in the two western bays of the north aisle. Marcel Dickson and Christiane Dickson, *Les Églises romanes de l'ancien diocèse de Chalon*, Mâcon, 1935, 231, without describing in specific detail the changes in vaulting, posited two campaigns for the church at Le Puley.

6. Francis Bond, *An Introduction to English Church Architecture*, London, 1913, 288–90.

7. For the date, construction, and bibliography of the nave of Saint-Philibert at Tournus, see C. Edson Armi, "The Nave of Saint-Philibert at Tournus," *Journal of the Society of Architectural Historians*, 60/1, 2001, 46–67, at 46–60.

8. Minott Kerr, "The Former Cluniac Priory Church of Paray-le-Monial: A Study of Its Architecture and Sculpture," Ph.D. diss., History of Art Dept., Yale University, 1994, 167.

9. For a discussion of Mozarabic arches and the historiography surrounding them, see José Fernández Arenas, *Mozarabic Architecture*, Greenwich, Conn., 1972, 154–6; for specific characteristics of the horseshoe arch in Catalonia, see Pierre Ponsich, "L'Art de bâtir en Roussillon et en Cerdagne du IXᵉ au XIIIᵉ siècle," *Les Cahiers de Saint-Michel-de-Cuxa* 26, 1995, 35–56, at 45–8; Xavier Barral i Altet, *L'art pre-romànic a Catalunya, segles IX–X*, Barcelona, 1981; Joan Badia i Homs, *L'arquitectura medieval de L'Empordà*, Girona, 2 vols., 1977, 1: 22–30; and Manuel Gómez Moreno, *Iglesias mozárabes: Arte español de los siglos IX a XI*, Madrid, 1919, 41–70. In tenth-century buildings like the chevet of Saint-Genis-des-Fontaines and nave and transept of Saint-Michel-de-Cuxa, masons created arcades with central voussoirs that are much longer than the voussoirs on the sides.

10. At Cluny III, the remaining outside wall of the southern aisle of the nave and choir was built in horizontal sections. Masons first built the wall to the level of the springing of the groin webs, and later, when they completed the construction of the freestanding piers, vaulted the outside aisle; see Armi, *Masons and Sculptors*, 157–69, figs. 57, 65.

11. For the related system of spines in Roman groin vaults, see Choisy, *Romains*, 76–80.

12. Kenneth John Conant, "Early Examples of the Pointed Arch and Vault in Romanesque Architecture," *Viator* 2, 1971, 203–9, at 207, proposed that the vertical angle of the arrises in the side-aisle vault of Cluny III reflects the shape of the formwork that was used: "Though rounded off at the base, the arrises are nearly straight over a large part of their length, as are the elements of the vault surface, so that the centering could be built up as a criss-cross of four planks, each rounded off a little at each end, and rising (one from each corner) to a mitre at the highest point."

CHAPTER FIVE: THE BARREL VAULT

1. For analysis of the construction of the vaults of the upper narthex of Saint-Philibert at Tournus, see Maurice Allemand, "La Construction du narthex de Saint-Philibert de Tournus," *Travaux des étudiants du groupe d'histoire de l'art de la Faculté des lettres de Paris*, 1928, 6–21; L. Barbier, "Études sur les voûtes du premier étage du narthex de Saint-Philibert de Tournus," *Bulletin monumental* 92, 1933, 51–7; and Edmond Malo, "Les Voûtes de la chapelle haute de l'église abbatiale de Tournus," *Bulletin monumental* 98, 1939, 73–84.

2. Antonio Almagro Gorbea, "La torre nazarí de Romilla: Análisis de una técnica constructiva," in Luigi Marino, ed., *Materiali da costruzione e tecniche edili antiche*, Florence, 1991, 19–22.

3. An architect, alone or in conjunction with a team of workers, could have designed parts of Saint-Philibert at Tournus (see the theory of Jacques Henriet, *Saint-Philibert de Tournus, l'abbatiale du XIᵉ siècle*, Paris, 1992). A capital supporting the arcade of the corbeled apse in the eastern end of the upper narthex depicts a bearded man holding in his left hand an ax or adz. Jean Virey, *Saint-Philibert de Tournus*, Paris, 1954, 35, and Jean Vallery-Radot, *Saint-Philibert de Tournus*, 1955, 209, concluded that this man was an architect, named in the stone inscription above his head: GERLANNUS ABATE ISTO MONETERIUM EILE (for an alternative transcription, see Virey, *Tournus*, 34). I agree with the opinion of Marcel Dickson and Christiane Dickson, *Les Églises romanes de l'ancien diocèse de Chalon*, Mâcon, 1935, 322, that the meaning of the Latin words "demeure assez obscur."

4. The practice of cantilevering the springing of a barrel vault was common in Byzantine brick buildings like the third-century basilica at Aspendos in Pamphylia; see David Talbot Rice, *The Great Palace of the Byzantine Emperors*, Edinburgh, 1958, 90, fig. 32,b.

5. The idea of using a half-barrel vault to support a full barrel vault is related to the structural solution in the upper story of the rotunda of Saint-Bénigne at Dijon; see Pierre de Truchis, "L'Architecture lombarde: Ses origines, son extension dans le centre, l'est et le midi de l'Europe," *Congrès archéologique* 76, 1909, 204–42, at 217.

6. John Fitchen, *The Construction of Gothic Cathedrals: A Study of Medieval Vault Erection*, Chicago, 1961, 108–21.

7. Kurt D. Alexander, Robert Mark, and John F. Abel, "The Structural Behavior of Medieval Ribbed Vaulting," *Journal of the Society of Architectural Historians* 36, 1977, 241–51.

8. The transverse arch in the western bay appears to be earlier than the transverse arches in the rest of the nave. Jordi Vigué, et al., "Sant Vicenç de Cardona," *Catalunya romànica*, vol. 11: *El Bages*, Barcelona, 1989, 151–71.

9. In the transept of the priory church of Semur-en-Brionnais, masons coursed the corbeled masonry in the lower portion of the barrel vault directly into the masonry of the window jambs.

CHAPTER SIX: SYSTEMS OF ARCH SUPPORT

1. C. Edson Armi, "The Corbel Table," *Gesta* 39/2, 2000, 89–116, at 99–102.

2. For a discussion of First Romanesque and classically based decoration, as opposed to structural systems, in Ottonian architecture, see Louis Grodecki, *L'Architecture ottonienne*, Paris, 1958, 262–71.

3. Marcel Dickson and Christiane Dickson, *Les Églises romanes de l'ancien diocèse de Chalon,* Mâcon, 1935, 320; Pierre de Truchis, "L'Architecture lombarde: Ses origines, son extension dans le centre, l'est et le midi de l'Europe," *Congrès archéologique* 76, 1909, 204–42, at 217. By corbeling the walls beneath the crossing dome, masons could reduce the width of the crossing, and thus save scaffolding and the complicated labor required to build a true vault, plus direct the thrust from the dome to descend more toward the center of the wall. Had they not cantilevered these surfaces and narrowed the distance between the walls below the dome, masons would have had to rest the vault above the crossing arches. This construction would have directed the thrust from the dome toward a less structurally effective location on the outside of the wall. None of these buildings has a transept, let alone a transept with a barrel vault, to support the weight from the dome. Had they not cantilevered the dome, therefore, masons would have had to increase substantially the width of the lateral outside walls of the crossing. In the twelfth century, in Provence masons continued to recognize the need for added lateral support in domical crossings in churches without transepts. In Notre-Dame-des-Doms in Avignon, for example, they used numerous, progressively larger discharging arches to secure the base of the squinched dome; see L.-H. Labande, "Avignon," *Congrès archéologique* 76, 1909, 6–16, and René Chappuis, "Églises romanes à coupole portée par deux ou trois étages d'arcs," *Bulletin monumental* 123, 1965, 295–314.

4. Jean Virey, *Les Églises romanes de l'ancien diocèse de Mâcon: Cluny et sa région,* Mâcon, 1935, 340–4.

5. Ibid., 331–5.

CHAPTER SEVEN: THE POINTED ARCH AND THE CONTEXT OF HIGH ROMANESQUE ARCHITECTURE IN BURGUNDY

1. L. Marini, "La chiesa romanica di S. Maria e S. Sigismondo a Rivolta d'Adda: Materiale per un'edizione critica," *Arte lombarda* 68, 1984, 5–26; Cesare Nava, *La chiesa di Rivolta d'Adda: Un monumento sconosciuto dell'architettura lombarda,* Milan, 1903. Jean Bony, *French Gothic Architecture of the 12th and 13th Centuries,* Berkeley and Los Angeles, 1983, 7, 465 n. 2, and idem, "Diagonality and Centrality in Early Rib-Vaulted Architectures," *Gesta* 15, 1976, 15–25, at 16: "The nave of Rivolta d'Adda is a typical example of that Lombard group. Vaulted in large domed units, each spanning two bays and roughly square in plan, this nave shows the application of a concept of strongly centered spaces in which the diagonal ribs become a further element of convergence, stressing the self-contained autonomy of the successive blocks of space." Other buildings of this type are Sant'Anastasio in Asti, Sant'Eustorgio in Milan, San Michele in Pavia, and the abbey church in San Nazzaro Sesia; see Adriano Peroni, "La struttura del S. Giovanni in Borgo di Pavia e il problema della copertura nell'architettura romanica lombarda," *Arte lombarda* 14/1, 1969, 21–34; 14/2, 1969, 63–76.

2. The vault, plan, articulation, and space in Roman baths and vaulted Early Christian basilicas may have inspired Lombard masons to explore domical vaults with round arches. Both the ribs in Sant'Ambrogio at Milan and the arrises in the Basilica of Maxentius in Rome rest on isolated supports between round-headed arches in square bays.

3. In contrast, early Lombard masons often used a small barrel vault in the choir.

4. Marie-Madeleine Jacquemet, *Église romane de Saint Martin de Laives, XIᵉ–XIIᵉ siècle en Bourgogne,* Chalon-sur-Saône, 1985.

5. For a photograph of an original Lombard band behind a later buttress on the exterior of the northern clerestory at Chapaize, see C. Edson Armi, "Report on the Destruction of Romanesque Architecture in Burgundy," *Journal of the Society of Architectural Historians* 55/3, 1996, 300–27, at 309, fig. 14.

6. See C. Edson Armi, "Saint-Philibert at Tournus and Wall Systems of First Romanesque Architecture," Ph.D. diss., Dept. of Art History and Archaeology, Columbia University, 1973, 26–7, for changes in the dimensions, foundations, and construction between the narthex and nave piers; Jean Martin, "Appendice," *Bulletin monumental* 67, 1903, 557–8.

7. C. Edson Armi, "The Nave of Saint-Philibert at Tournus," *Journal of the Society of Architectural Historians* 60/1, 2001, 46–67.

8. L. Barbier, "Études sur les voûtes du premier étage du narthex de Saint-Philibert de Tournus," *Bulletin monumental* 92, 1933, 51–7, at 56, understood the important role of the eastern walls under the western towers in dispersing weight from the vault in the central vessel of the upper narthex at Tournus. In contrast, Edmond Malo, "Les Voûtes de la chapelle haute de l'église abbatiale de Tournus," *Bulletin monumental* 98, 1939, 73–84, in his calculations seems to have overlooked the role of the tower as a support. Barbier perceptively observed the unusual layout of the stones in the central and aisle vaults, but he did not mention possible constructive, as opposed to structural, explanations for this design. I believe he is not entirely accurate in his structural analysis of the stones in these vaults (see also E. Ranquet and H. Ranquet, "Origine française du berceau roman," *Bulletin monumental* 90, 1931, 35–74, at 55). Once laid, individual stones would not have had a major impact on each other, but instead would have tended to act together with the mortar to form a shell. In the case of a thin shell, the type and direction of stone coursing is incidental to the action of the vault. Whether the builders were aware of the structural properties of thin-shell construction is, of course, another question. Also, I think Barbier may not totally be accurate in dismissing a structural role for the transverse arches in supporting the central vault and bracing the wall beneath it. There is very little evidence in favor of his conclusion that the builders were aware of this limitation: "[L]e constructeur des voûtes du premier étage du narthex de Saint-Philibert de Tournus savait que les doubleaux des berceaux ne servent généralement que de cintres permanents limitant les fissures et les déformations."

9. Armi, "Corbel Table," 114 n. 52.

10. In the twelfth century, masons replaced the round-headed barrel vault with a pointed one.

11. J. E. Gordon, *Structures, or Why Things Don't Fall Down*, Aylesbury, 1978, 175–81.

12. This exceptionally low arch is the result of the decision by masons to place a door to the nave in each aisle of the upper narthex. To allow direct access from the upper narthex into the nave, in each side aisle of the upper narthex they created a diagonal portal that penetrates the eastern corner of the outside wall (see Fig. 68). To make room for this diagonal portal, in each eastern bay they splayed the aisle wall. Having narrowed the width of the aisle in this manner, they had to narrow, and thus to lower, the half-barrel vault that rests on top of the splayed wall. Once they decided to reduce the circumference of the vault, not enough space remained between the underside of the vault and the top of the portal to stilt the springing of the arch. On the chapel opening in the center of the eastern wall of the upper narthex, see Christian Sapin, "L'Ouverture est de la chapelle

Saint-Michel de Tournus," *Société des Amis des Arts et des Sciences de Tournus* 86, 1987, 149–51.

13. In no brick-based church in southern Burgundy did masons copy the Tournus system of lateral barrel vaults; see Walter Berry, "Le Système de voûtement de la nef de Saint-Philibert de Tournus dans son contexte régional," in *Saint-Philibert de Tournus: Histoire, archéologie, art. Actes du colloque du Centre International d'Études Romanes, Tournus, 15–19 juin 1994*, Mâcon, 1995, 297–321.

14. On the related issue of longitudinal thrust in sexpartite-vault construction, see Robert Mark, *Light, Wind, and Structure: The Mystery of the Master Builders*, Cambridge, Mass., 1990, 117; R. Mark and E. C. Robison, "Vaults and Domes," in Robert Mark, *Architectural Technology up to the Scientific Revolution*, Cambridge, Mass., 1993, 138–81, at 156–9.

15. Jean Virey, *Les Églises romanes de l'ancien diocèse de Mâcon: Cluny et sa région*, Mâcon, 1935, 376–87.

16. It remains a question whether masons began Saint-Hippolyte before 1088, when construction was begun on Cluny III; see C. Edson Armi, *Masons and Sculptors in Romanesque Burgundy: The New Aesthetic of Cluny III*, University Park, Pa., 1983, 51–2. Masons built the nave of Saint-Hippolyte using an almost entirely brick-based technique. The only exceptions to this technique can be found in details like the diagonal chamfer on the side of imposts and the slightly enlarged trapezoidal stones around arcades and openings. Particularly on the northern aisle wall, but also throughout the nave, masons interspersed masonry beds with the stone equivalent of brick headers. In Lombardy, masons often used this technique to key brick courses into the fabric of the wall; stones shaped like brick headers can also be found in the clerestory of Saint-Philibert at Tournus and in the chapel of Saint-Laurent at Cotte.

17. Virey, *Les Églises romanes*, 378, fig. 23.

18. For a plan of the original parts of Gigny, see Christian Sapin, "L'Abbatiale de Gigny," in Annick Richard and Claudine Munier, eds., *Éclats d'histoire: 10 ans d'archéologie en Franche-Comté, 2500 ans d'héritages*, Besançon, 1995, 372–3.

19. French and international, not local Burgundian, prototypes usually are cited as the sources for the elevation of Cluny; see Armi, *Masons and Sculptors*, 24–9.

20. For the dates of Paray-le-Monial, see Minott Kerr, "The Former Cluniac Priory Church of Paray-le-Monial: A Study of Its Architecture and Sculpture," Ph.D. diss., History of Art Dept., Yale University, 1994, 224–90.

21. In the nave of Cluny III illustrated by Giffart, flying buttresses do not reach the very top of the clerestory (see Fig. 125); the upper part of the original buttresses can be discerned in the space below the eaves. In the choir of Cluny III, this engraving also shows the original pattern of one flat buttress projecting between two narrow pilasters. Masons repeated this pattern in the chevet at Paray-le-Monial.

22. On the relation of the alignment of the foundations of the aisle walls of Cluny III to pressure from the vaults of the crossing, see Anne Baud and Gilles Rollier, "Abbaye de Cluny: Campagne archéologique 1991–1992," *Bulletin monumental* 151/3, 1993, 429–68, at 464.

23. The joining of the transverse clerestory vaults with an ashlar framework to relieve the weight of a longitudinal barrel may have been a continuation of experiments undertaken by masons (who were closely associated with the ambulatory capitals at Cluny III) on the clerestory arcades of the ruined Cluniac abbey church of Saint-Fortunat at Charlieu; see C. Edson Armi, "The Charlieu Clerestory and the Brionnais Sources for Cluny III," *Gesta* 25, 1986, 49–60. Consecrated in 1094,

shortly after Cluny III was begun, the church at Charlieu was one of the most important southern Burgundian buildings preceding the mother church. Its nave –
like that of Cluny III – originally combined a longitudinal barrel with three ashlar
clerestory arcades per bay; see Elizabeth R. Sunderland, *Charlieu à l'époque médiévale*, Lyons, 1971, 41–7. The two side arcades in the clerestory at Charlieu, like
those in the second stories at Cluny and Paray, probably were blind. The Cluny-
related masons at Charlieu conceived this arcaded ashlar clerestory in response
to a relatively small-scale problem: to build a two-story, round-arch structure, in
which groin webs on either side of the nave transfer the weight from the central
vault directly to buttresses outside the aisles. Later, at the abbey churches at Cluny
and Paray, masons faced a more difficult challenge: to relay the weight from a
higher central barrel vault down three stories and across two aisles. To meet this
new challenge, they expanded the size, number, and location of lateral arcades in
the elevation.

24. In the transept of Cluny III, masons used only an ashlar facing in the second-story blind arcade. According to Kenneth J. Conant, "Five Old Prints of the
Abbey Church of Cluny," *Speculum* 3, 1928, 401–4, at 404, "[i]t seems likely that
during the seventeenth or eighteenth century two out of the three original windows in each bay of the clearstory were blocked up in order to strengthen the
high vault."

25. For debate on this issue, see Armi, "Corbel Table," n. 75.

26. For the debate whether masons vaulted the choir of Cluny III with semicircular or pointed-barrel vaults, see ibid., n. 68.

27. For a discussion of local sources for the three-story elevation, see Armi, *Masons and Sculptors*, 56. It may have taken almost a century and the aid of flying
buttresses for masons to revive the Cluny III concept of a three-story skeletal
elevation with lateral barrel vaults on the upper two stories. As in Cluny III, in
the cathedral at Chartres masons used a proportionally high nave arcade to open
the view on the ground floor; this ground-story void was made possible by support from a series of transverse triforium vaults and a transverse barrel vault surrounding each clerestory window which, as at Cluny III, descends well below the
springing of the nave vault.

28. Masons frequently coordinated the courses of brick-based infill with the
vertical dimensions of the ashlar in the responds and buttresses. See Anne Baud,
"La Maior Ecclesia de Cluny: Un Exemple de construction horizontale," *Dossiers
d'archéologie* 251, 2000, 34–5; Nicolas Reveyron, "Culture technique et architecture
monumentale: Analyse structurelle des types de contrefort dans l'architecture romane," in Patrice Beck, ed., *L'Innovation technique au Moyen Âge: Actes du VIe congrès
international d'archéologie médiévale, 1–5 octobre 1996, Dijon*, Paris, 1998, 211–18, at
216–17.

29. At Cluny III in 1125, a vault did collapse. This unlocated calamity may indicate that masons overestimated the strength of the structure of Cluny III. On the
differing theories about the collapse of this vault, see Armi, "Corbel Table," n. 65.

CONCLUSION

1. Roger Stalley, *Early Medieval Architecture*, Oxford, 1999, 134, criticized the as-
sumption that medieval methods of vaulting followed a neat typological progression.

Bibliography

Abadal i de Vinyals, Ramon d'. *Els primers comtes catalans.* Barcelona, 1958.

Abadal i de Vinyals, Ramon d', Jordi Rubió, Ferran Soldevila, Miquel Tarradell, and J. Vicens Vives. *Moments crucials de la història de Catalunya.* Barcelona, 1962.

Acland, John H. *Medieval Structure: The Gothic Vault.* Toronto, 1972.

Agnelli, Giovanni, ed. *Piemonte, Valle d'Aosta.* Milan, 1968.

Alexander, Kurt D., Robert Mark, and John F. Abel. "The Structural Behavior of Medieval Ribbed Vaulting." *Journal of the Society of Architectural Historians* 36, 1977, 241–51.

Allemand, Maurice. "La Construction du narthex de Saint-Philibert de Tournus." *Travaux des étudiants du groupe d'histoire de l'art de la Faculté des lettres de Paris,* 1928, 6–21.

Amédée, Paul, ed. *Encyclopédie de l'architecture et de la construction.* Paris, 1888.

Armi, C. Edson. "Saint-Philibert at Tournus and Wall Systems of First Romanesque Architecture." Ph.D. diss., Dept. of Art History and Archaeology, Columbia University, 1973. Available (1975) from UMI Dissertation Services, Ann Arbor, Mich.

"Orders and Continuous Orders in Romanesque Architecture." *Journal of the Society of Architectural Historians* 34, 1975, 178–88.

Masons and Sculptors in Romanesque Burgundy: The New Aesthetic of Cluny III. University Park, Pa., 1983.

"The Charlieu Clerestory and the Brionnais Sources for Cluny III." *Gesta* 25, 1986, 49–60.

"Report on the Destruction of Romanesque Architecture in Burgundy." *Journal of the Society of Architectural Historians* 55/3, 1996, 300–27.

"The Corbel Table." *Gesta* 39/2, 2000, 89–116.

"The Nave of Saint-Philibert at Tournus." *Journal of the Society of Architectural Historians,* 60/1, 2001, 46–67.

Arslan, Edoardo. "L'architettura dalla conquista longobarda al 1000"; "L'architettura romanica milanese." *Storia di Milano.* Milan, 1954, 2: 501–608; 3: 397–521.

"Les Églises lombardes du VIᵉ au Xᵉ siècle." *Comptes rendus de l'Académie des Inscriptions et Belles-Lettres,* 1954, 165–70.

Ascoli, G. I. "Schizzi franco-provenzali." *Archivio glottologico italiano* 3, 1878, 61–120.

Aubert, Marcel. "Les Plus Anciennes Croisées d'ogives: Leur rôle dans la construction." *Bulletin monumental* 93, 1934, 5–67, 137–237.

Badia i Homs, Joan. *L'arquitectura medieval de L'Empordà*. Girona, 2 vols. (1: *Baix Empordà*; 2: *Alt Empordà*), 1977.

Barbier, L. "Études sur les voûtes du premier étage du narthex de Saint-Philibert de Tournus." *Bulletin monumental* 92, 1933, 51–7.

Barocelli, P. *La strada e le costruzioni romane della Alpis Graia*. Turin, 1924.

Barral i Altet, Xavier. *L'art pre-romànic a Catalunya, segles IX–X*. Barcelona, 1981.

   ed. *Le Paysage monumental de la France autour de l'an mil: Colloque international C.N.R.S., Hugues Capet 987–1987: La France de l'an mil, juin–septembre 1987*. Paris, 1987.

Baud, Anne. "La Maior Ecclesia de Cluny: Un Exemple de construction horizontale." *Dossiers d'archéologie* 251, 2000, 34–5.

Baud, Anne, and Gilles Rollier. "Abbaye de Cluny: Campagne archéologique 1991–1992." *Bulletin monumental* 151/3, 1993, 429–68.

Bec, Pierre. *La Langue occitane*. Paris, 1967.

Beck, Patrice, ed. *L'Innovation technique au Moyen Âge: Actes du VIᵉ congrès international d'archéologie médiévale, 1–5 octobre 1996, Dijon*. Paris, 1998.

Benvenuto, Edoardo, Massimo Corradi, and Federico Foce. "Sintesi storica sulla statica di archi, volte e cupole nel XIX secolo." *Palladio* n.s. 1/2, 1988, 52–68.

Bergier, Jean-Françoise. "Géographie des cols alpins à la fin du Moyen Âge: Quelques remarques d'ordre méthodologique et chronologique sur le trafic alpin." *Bulletin Annuel de la Fondation Suisse* 4, 1955, 11–27.

Bernardi, Attilio. *Chiese romaniche del Cantone Ticino*. Torno, 1968.

Berry, Walter. "Le Système de voûtement de la nef de Saint-Philibert de Tournus dans son contexte régional." In Jacques Thirion, ed., *Saint-Philibert de Tournus: Histoire, archéologie, art. Actes du colloque du Centre International d'Études Romanes, Tournus, 15–19 juin 1994*. Mâcon, 1995, 297–321.

Bertelli, M. Carlo, ed. *Il millennio ambrosiano: La città del vescovo dai Carolingi al Barbarossa*. Milan, 1988.

Berton, R. *Les Châteaux du Val d'Aoste*. Aosta, 1950.

   Les Monuments moyenâgeux de la cité d'Aoste. Aosta, 1952.

Bessac, J.-C., F. Journot, D. Prigent, C. Sapin, and J. Seigne. *La Construction: La Pierre*. Paris, 1999.

Binding, Günther. *Baubetrieb im Mittelalter*. Darmstadt, 1993.

Blanchard, Raoul. *Les Alpes occidentales*. Grenoble, 7 vols., 1941–56.

Blanchet, Adrien. *L'Archéologie gallo-romaine*. Paris, 1935.

Bligny, Bernard. *L'Église et les ordres religieux dans le royaume de Bourgogne aux XIᵉ et XIIᵉ siècles*. Grenoble, 1960.

Bois, Guy. *The Transformation of the Year One Thousand: The Village of Lournand from Antiquity to Feudalism*. Manchester, 1992.

Bognetti, G., and C. Marcora. *L'abbazia benedettina di Civate*. Lecco, 1957.

Bond, Francis. *An Introduction to English Church Architecture*. London, 1913.

Bonnassie, Pierre. *La Catalogne au tournant de l'an mil: Croissance et mutations d'une société*. Paris, 1990.

   From Slavery to Feudalism in Southwestern Europe. Cambridge, 1991.

Bonnery, André. "Premières manifestations de l'architecture romane en Languedoc méditerranéen: Les Églises abbatiales." *Les Cahiers de Saint-Michel-de-Cuxa* 21, 1990, 75–93.

Bony, Jean. "Diagonality and Centrality in Early Rib-Vaulted Architectures." *Gesta* 15, 1976, 15–25.

French Gothic Architecture of the 12th and 13th Centuries. Berkeley and Los Angeles, 1983.

Bourciez, Édouard. *Éléments de linguistique romane.* Paris, 1923.

Branner, Robert. *Burgundian Gothic Architecture.* London, 1960.

Brooke, Christopher. *Europe in the Central Middle Ages.* Essex, 2000.

Brune, Paul. "Les Églises romanes du Jura"; "L'Architecture religieuse dans le Jura." *Congrès archéologique* 58, 1891, 152–76, 353–64.

Brutails, Jean-Auguste. *Précis d'archéologie du Moyen Âge.* Toulouse, 1936.

Bulst, Neithard. "Guillaume de Dijon, le bâtisseur de la rotonde." In Monique Jannet and Christian Sapin, eds., *Guillaume de Volpiano et l'architecture des rotondes: Actes de colloque* (Dijon, 23–25 septembre 1993). Dijon, 1996, 19–29.

Canova dal Zio, Regina. *Le chiese delle Tre Venezie anteriori al mille.* Padua, 1986.

Capra, Raul. *La basilica di S. Michele in Oleggio.* Novara, 1968.

Carratelli, Giovanni Pugliese, ed. *Magistra Barbaritas: I Barbari in Italia.* Milan, 1984.

Cattaneo, Enrico. *Terra di Sant'Ambrogio.* Milan, 1989.

Cattaneo, Enrico, and F. Reggiori. *La basilica di S. Ambrogio.* Milan, 1966.

Cecchi, Roberto. "San Lorenzo Maggiore tra XI e XII secolo: Alcuni aspetti costruttivi." In Carlo Bertelli, ed., *Il millennio ambrosiano: La città del vescovo dai Carolingi al Barbarossa.* Milan, 1988, 176–95.

Chappuis, René. "Églises romanes à coupole portée par deux ou trois étages d'arcs." *Bulletin monumental* 123, 1965, 295–314.

"Utilisation du tracé ovale dans l'architecture des églises romanes." *Bulletin monumental* 134, 1976, 7–36.

Chaume, Maurice. *Les Origines du duché de Bourgogne.* Dijon, 4 vols., 1925–37.

Chédeville, André, Jacques Le Goff, and Jacques Rossiaud. *La Ville en France au Moyen Âge.* Paris, 1998.

Chierici, Gino. *La chiesa di S. Satiro a Milano e alcune considerazioni sull'architettura preromanica in Lombardia.* Milan, 1942.

"La chiesa di S. Maria Maggiore a Lomello." *Palladio* 1, 1951, 67–93.

Chierici, Sandro. *Lombardie romane.* Pierre-qui-vire, 1978.

Piémont-Ligurie roman. Pierre-qui-vire, 1979.

Chierici, Umberto. *Il battistero del Duomo di Novara.* Milan, 1967.

"Fra cultura padana e cultura francese." In Giovanni Agnelli, ed., *Piemonte, Valle d'Aosta.* Milan, 1968, 352–3.

Choisy, Auguste. *L'Art de bâtir chez les Romains.* Paris, 1873.

L'Art de bâtir chez les Byzantins. Paris, 1883.

Histoire de l'architecture. Paris, 2 vols., 1929.

Cluny, un nouveau regard: Recherches archéologiques 1988–1995; Présentation des fouilles récentes par A. Baud et G. Rollier, Musée d'Art et d'Archéologie. Cluny, 1996.

Coldstream, Nicola. *Medieval Craftsmen: Masons and Sculptors.* London, 1991.

Colombier, Pierre du. *Les Chantiers des cathédrales: Ouvriers, architectes, sculpteurs.* Paris, 1973.

Conant, Kenneth J[ohn]. "Five Old Prints of the Abbey Church of Cluny." *Speculum* 3, 1928, 401–4.

A Brief Commentary on Early Medieval Architecture. Baltimore, 1942.

"Observations on the Vaulting Problems of the Period 1088–1211." *Gazette des beaux-arts* 6/26, 1944, 127–34.

Carolingian and Romanesque Architecture 800 to 1200. Baltimore, 1959.

Cluny, les églises et la maison du chef d'ordre. Mâcon, 1968.

"Early Examples of the Pointed Arch and Vault in Romanesque Architecture." *Viator* 2, 1971, 203–9.

Conrad, Dietrich. *Kirchenbau im Mittelalter: Bauplanung und Bauausführung.* Leipzig, 1990.

Cope, Christopher. *Phoenix Frustrated: The Lost Kingdom of Burgundy.* London, 1986.

Dard, Charles. *Farges-les-Mâcon.* Mâcon, 1927.

Dartein, Fernand de. *Étude sur l'architecture lombarde et sur les origines de l'architecture romano-byzantine: Atlas des planches.* Paris, 1865–82.

Daugas, Jean-Pierre, ed. *L'Échafaudage dans le chantier médiéval.* Documents d'archéologie en Rhône-Alpes 13. Lyons (Ministère de la Culture/DRAC-SRA), 1996.

Dauzat, Albert. *La Géographie linguistique.* Paris, 1922.

Davey, Norman. *A History of Building Materials.* London, 1961.

Decour, Armand. *Le Patois de Bettant: Généralités extraits de la grammaire, curiosités.* Mantes, 1966.

Deichmann, Friedrich Wilhelm. *Studien zur Architektur Konstantinopels.* Mainz, 1954.

Delage, A. *La Vie économique et sociale de la Bourgogne dans le Haut Moyen Âge.* Mâcon, 3 vols., 1941.

Delcor, Mathias. "Joseph Puig i Cadafalch, historien de l'art roman." *Les Cahiers de Saint-Michel-de-Cuxa* 16, 1985, 25–50.

Della Valle, E. *Agliate, basilica e battistero.* Seregno, 1958.

Delort, Robert, ed. *La France de l'an mil.* Paris, 1990.

Derand, P. François. *L'Architecture des voûtes, ou l'art des traits et coupe des voûtes.* Paris, 1643.

Deshoulières, François. *Au début de l'art roman: Les Églises de l'XIe siècle en France.* Paris, 1929.

Dickson, Marcel, and Christiane Dickson. *Les Églises romanes de l'ancien diocèse de Chalon.* Mâcon, 1935.

Dodds, Jerrilynn D. *Architecture and Ideology in Early Medieval Spain.* University Park, Pa., 1990.

Dondaine, Colette. *Les Parlers comtois d'oïl: Étude phonétique.* Paris, 1972.

Duby, Georges. *Guerriers et paysans, VII–XIIe siècle: Premier essor de l'économie européenne.* Paris, 1973.

L'An mil. Paris, 1980.

La Société aux XIe et XIIe siècles dans la région mâconnaise. Paris, [1953] 1982.

Féodalité. Paris, 1996.

Art and Society in the Middle Ages. Cambridge, 2000.

Duckett, Eleanor. *Death and Life in the Tenth Century.* Ann Arbor, 1967.

Duhem, Gustave. "Église Saint-Désiré de Lons-le-Saunier." *Congrès archéologique* 118, 1960, 176–88.

Duparc, Pierre. *Le Comté de Genève IXe–XVe siècle.* Geneva, 1955.

Durand-Claye, A. "Notes sur la vérification de la stabilité des voûtes en maçonnerie et sur l'emploi des courbes de pression." *Annales des ponts et chaussées* 12, 1867, 63–96.

Durliat, Marcel. "Problèmes posés par l'histoire de l'architecture religieuse en Catalogne dans la première moitié du XIe siècle." *Les Cahiers de Saint-Michel-de-Cuxa* 3, 1972, 43–9.

"La Méditerranée et l'art roman." *Les Cahiers de Saint-Michel-de-Cuxa* 6, 1975, 107–16.

"La Catalogne et le 'premier art roman'." *Bulletin monumental* 147/3, 1989, 209–38.

Duvernoy, René. *Les Églises de Franche-Comté*. Strasbourg, 1976.

Enlart, Camille. *Manuel d'archéologie française depuis les temps mérovingiens jusqu'à la Renaissance*. Paris, 3 vols., 1919.

Escoffier, Simone. *La Rencontre de la langue d'oïl, de la langue d'oc et du francoprovençal entre Loire et Allier: Limites phonétiques et morphologiques*. Paris, 1958.

Farreras, Joaquim Nadal, and Philippe Wolff, eds. *Histoire de la Catalogne*. Toulouse, 1982.

Febvre, Lucien. *Histoire de Franche-Comté*. Paris, 1932.

Fernández Arenas, José. *Mozarabic Architecture*. Greenwich, Conn., 1972.

Ferrero, Daria de Bernardi. "Aoste, la cathédrale de Sainte-Marie"; "Ivrée, la cathédrale de Sainte-Marie." *Congrès archéologique* 129, 1978, 157–72, 185–93.

Fiétier, Roland, ed. *Histoire de la Franche-Comté: Naissance et essor du Comté (XIe–XIIIe siècle)*. Toulouse, 1977.

Finocchi, Anna. *L'architettura romanica nel territorio di Varese*. Milan, 1966.

Fitchen, John. *The Construction of Gothic Cathedrals: A Study of Medieval Vault Erection*. Chicago, 1961.

Focillon, Henri. *The Art of the West in the Middle Ages*. London and New York, 2 vols., 1969.

The Year 1000. New York, 1969.

Forneris, Giuliana. *Romanico in terra d'Arduino*. Ivrea, 1978.

Fossier, Robert. *Enfance de l'Europe Xe–XIIe siècles: Aspects économiques et sociaux*. Paris, 2 vols., 1982.

Peasant Life in the Medieval West. London, 1988.

La Société médiévale. Paris, 1991.

Villages et villageois au Moyen Âge. Paris, 1995.

Fourquin, Guy. *Lordship and Feudalism in the Middle Ages*. London, 1976.

Galassi, Giuseppe. "Il campanile di Baggio e gli archetipi delle torri lombarde." *Palladio* 1, 1951, 70–7.

Gall, Ernst, "Die Abteikirche Saint-Philibert in Tournus, eine kritische Untersuchung zur frühburgundischen Baukunst." *Der Cicerone* 4, 1912, 624–36.

"St. Philibert in Tournus." *Zeitschrift für Kunstgeschichte* 15, 1952, 179–82.

Gardette, Pierre. *Études de géographie linguistique*. Strasbourg, 1983.

Garmier, Jean-François. *Le Guide du Mâconnais*. Paris, 1990.

Gaspard, B. *Histoire de Gigny*. Lons-le-Saunier, 1843.

Gilardoni, Virgilio, ed. *I monumenti d'arte e di storia del Canton Ticino*. Basel, 3 vols., 1972–83.

Giuliani, Cairoli Fulvio, and Roberto Marta. *Tecnica costruttiva a Roma nel medioevo*. Rome, 1989.

Glück, Heinrich. "Zur Entstehung der Gurten- und Rippengewölbes." *Belvedere* 9–10, 1926, 186–200.

Der Ursprung des römischen und abendländischen Wölbungsbaues. Vienna, 1933.

Goff, Jacques le, ed. *Histoire de la France religieuse: Des dieux de la Gaule à la papauté d'Avignon*. Paris, 1988.

Gómez Moreno, Manuel. *Iglesias mozárabes: Arte español de los siglos IX a XI*. Madrid, 1919.

Gorbea, Antonio Almagro. "La torre nazarí de Romilla: Análisis de una técnica constructiva." In Luigi Marino, ed., *Materiali da costruzione e tecniche edili antiche*. Florence, 1991, 19–22.

Gordon, J. E. *Structures, or Why Things Don't Fall Down*. Aylesbury, 1978.

Grenier, Albert. *Manuel d'archéologie gallo-romaine, 2e partie: Les Routes*. Paris, 1934.

Grodecki, Louis. *L'Architecture ottoniene.* Paris, 1958.
　Gothic Architecture. New York, 1976.
Gros, Chanoine Adolphe, and Chanoine Louis Gros. *Histoire de Maurienne.* Chambéry, 6 vols. (vols. 1–4, Adolphe; vols. 5–6, Louis), 1946–8, 1955, 1960.
Grütter, Max. "Die romanischen Kirchen am Thunersee: Ein Beitrag zur Frage der Ausbreitung frühlombardischer Architektur." *Anzeiger für schweizerische Altertumskunde,* 34, 1932, 118–37.
　Tausendjährige Kirchen am Thuner- und Brinzersee. Bern, 1956.
Guerreau, Alain. "Vingt et une petites églises romanes du Mâconnais: Irrégularités et métrologie." In Patrice Beck, ed., *L'Innovation technique au Moyen Âge: Actes du VIᵉ congrès international d'archéologie médiévale, 1–5 octobre 1996, Dijon.* Paris, 1998, 186–210.
Haeedah, Laleh. "Les Arcs brisés persans: Remarques sur leurs particularités géometriques et techniques." *Histoire de l'art* 11, 1990, 3–13.
Hall, Robert A., Jr., "The Linguistic Position of Franco-Provençal," *Language [Journal of the Linguistic Society of America]* 25, 1949, 1–14.
Hartmann-Virnich, Andreas. "L'Escalier en vis voûté et la construction romane: Exemples rhodaniens." *Bulletin monumental* 154/2, 1996, 113–28.
Helm, Sebastian, Ulrike Bangert-Laule, Bernhard Laule, and Heinfried Wischermann. *Saint-Philibert in Tournus: Baugeschichte und architekturgeschichtliche Stellung.* Freiburg, 1988.
Henriet, Jacques. *Saint-Philibert de Tournus, l'abbatiale du XIᵉ siècle.* Paris, 1992.
Hubert, Jean. "La Crypte de Saint-Jean-de-Maurienne et l'expansion de l'art lombard en France." *Bulletin de la Société Nationale des Antiquaires de France,* 1961, 40–9.
Iogna-Prat, Dominique. "Saint Maïeul de Cluny, le provençal entre histoire et légende." In Dominique Iogna-Prat, Barbara H. Rosenwein, Xavier Barral i Altet, and Guy Barruol, *Saint Maïeul, Cluny et la Provence: Expansion d'une abbaye à l'aube du Moyen Âge.* Mane, 1994, 7–14.
Iogna-Prat, Dominique, and Jean-Charles Picard. *Religion et culture autour de l'an mil: Royaume capétien et Lotharingie. Actes du colloque Hugues Capet 987–1987: La France de l'an mil, Auxerre 26 et 27 juin 1987.* Picard, 1990.
Jacquemet, Marie-Madeleine. *Église romane de Saint Martin de Laives, XIᵉ–XIIᵉ siècle en Bourgogne.* Chalon-sur-Saône, 1985.
Janin, Bernard. *Une Région alpine originale: Le Val d'Aoste, tradition et renouveau.* Grenoble, 1968.
Jannet, Monique, and Christian Sapin. *Guillaume de Volpiano et l'architecture des rotondes: Actes de colloque* (Dijon, 23–25 septembre 1993). Dijon, 1996.
Jeannin, Yves. "Franche-Comté: Orientations de l'archéologie." In Xavier Barral i Altet, ed., *Le Paysage monumental de la France autour de l'an mil: Colloque international C.N.R.S., Hugues Capet 987–1987: La France de l'an mil, juin–septembre 1987.* Paris, 1987, 327–31.
Jochnowitz, George. *Dialect Boundaries and the Question of Franco-Provençal.* The Hague, 1973.
Kerr, Minott. "The Former Cluniac Priory Church of Paray-le-Monial: A Study of Its Architecture and Sculpture." Ph.D. diss., History of Art Dept., Yale University, 1994. Available from UMI Dissertation Services, Ann Arbor, Mich. Also available in part at http://www.reed.edu/~mkerr/papers/thesis/t-list.html.
Kimpel, Dieter, and Robert Suckale. *Die gotische Architektur in Frankreich 1130–1270.* Munich, 1985.

Krautheimer, Richard. *Early Christian and Byzantine Architecture*. Baltimore, 1986.

Labande, L.-H. "Avignon." *Congrès archéologique* 76, 1909, 6–16.

Lacroix, Pierre. *Églises jurassiennes romanes et gothiques: Histoire et architecture*. Besançon, 1981.

Lamboglia, Nino. *I monumenti medioevali della Liguria di Ponente*. Turin, 1970.

Lauranson-Rosaz, Christian. "La Romanité du Midi de l'an mil." In Robert Delort, ed. *La France de l'an mil*. Paris, 1990, 49–73.

Lasteyrie, Robert de. *L'Architecture religieuse en France à l'époque romane*. Paris, 1929.

Lefèvre-Pontalis, Eugène. *Les Voûtes en berceau et d'arêtes sans doubleaux*. Paris, 1921.

Lemerle, Paul. *Philippes et la Macédoine orientale à l'époque chrétienne et byzantine: Recherches d'histoire et d'archéologie*. Paris, 1945.

Lopez, Robert S. *The Birth of Europe*. New York, 1966.

MacDonald, William Lloyd. *The Architecture of the Roman Empire*. New Haven, 1982.

Magenta, Gian Franco. *Le chiese di Lomello*. Vigevano, 1999.

Magni, Mariaclotilde. *Architettura romanica comasca*. Milan, 1960.

"Le torri campanarie romaniche nel Canton Ticino." *Commentari* 17, 1966, 28–43.

"Sopravvivenze carolinge e ottoniane nell'architettura romanica dell'arco alpino centrale." *Arte lombarda* 14/1, 1969, 35–44; 14/2, 1969, 77–87.

Architettura religiosa e scultura romanica nella Valle d'Aosta. Aosta, 1974.

"Un Remarquable Témoignage du premier art roman en Italie du nord: La Cathédrale d'Aoste." *Cahiers archéologiques* 24, 1975, 163–72.

Magnien, Émile. *Histoire de Mâcon et du Mâconnais*. Mâcon, 1971.

Malacart, Anna Segagni. "La 'Torre Civica' di Pavia e le torri campanarie padane del secolo XI." *Arte medievale* 4/2, 1990, 99–121.

Malo, Edmond. "Les Voûtes de la chapelle haute de l'église abbatiale de Tournus." *Bulletin monumental* 98, 1939, 73–84.

Malone, C. Marino. "Les Fouilles de Saint-Bénigne de Dijon (1976–78) et le problème de l'église de l'an mil." *Bulletin monumental* 138, 1980, 253–92.

Mango, Cyril. *Byzantine Architecture*. New York, 1976.

Marchetti, Leopoldo, ed. *Novara e il suo territorio*. Novara, 1952.

Marini, L. "La chiesa romanica di S. Maria e S. Sigismondo a Rivolta d'Adda: Materiale per un'edizione critica." *Arte lombarda* 68, 1984, 5–26.

Mark, Robert. *Experiments in Gothic Structure*. Cambridge, Mass., 1982.

Light, Wind, and Structure: The Mystery of the Master Builders. Cambridge, Mass., 1990.

ed. *Architectural Technology up to the Scientific Revolution: The Art and Structure of Large-Scale Buildings*. Cambridge, Mass., 1993.

Marti, F. Galtier. "L'Église ligurienne San Paragorio de Noli et ses rapports avec Santa Maria de Obarra (Aragon) et San Vicente de Cardona (Catalogne): Trois précoces témoignages artistiques de la 'diaspora' lombarde." *Cahiers de Saint-Michel-de-Cuxa* 19, 1988, 151–68.

Martin, Jean. "Appendice." *Bulletin monumental* 67, 1903, 557–8.

Moyse, Gérard. "Les origines du monachisme dans le diocèse de Besançon (V^e–Xe siècles)." *Bibliothèque de l'École des chartes* 131, 1973, 21–104, 369–485.

Nava, Cesare. *La chiesa di Rivolta d'Adda: Un monumento sconosciuto dell'architettura lombarda*. Milan, 1903.

Oursel, Charles. *L'Art roman de Bourgogne: Études d'histoire et d'archéologie*. Dijon, 1928.

Oursel, Raymond. *Art en Savoie.* Paris, 1975.

"Tableau de la Bresse romane." In René Tournier, ed., *Franche-Comté romane.* Pierre-qui-vire, 1979, 273–86.

Ottoway, John. "Traditions architecturales dans le nord de la France pendant le premier millénaire." *Cahiers de civilisation médiévale* 23/2, 1980, 141–72.

Panazza, Gaetano. *L'arte medioevale nel territorio bresciano.* Bergamo, 1942.

"Campanili romanici di Pavia." *Arte lombarda* 2, 1956, 18–27.

Perogalli, Carlo. "Chiese ad archi trasversi in Lombardia." *Arte lombarda* 38, 1993, 176–81.

Peroni, Adriano. "La cripta di Sant'Eusebio: Problemi e prospettive di un restauro in corso." *Pavia,* May–June 1968, 1–26.

"La struttura del S. Giovanni in Borgo di Pavia e il problema della copertura nell'architettura romanica lombarda." *Arte lombarda* 14/1, 1969, 21–34; 14/2, 1969, 63–76.

"Architettura dell'Italia settentrionale in epoca longobarda (problemi e prospettive)." *Corso di cultura sull'arte ravennate e bizantina. Seminario internazionale di studi sul tema: "Ravenna e l'Italia fra Goti e Longobardi"* 36, 1989, 323–45.

"Arte dell'XI secolo: Il ruolo di Milano e dell'area lombarda nel quadro europeo." *Atti dell'XI Congresso internazionale di studi sull'alto medioevo.* Spoleto, 1989, 751–81.

"Le Décor monumental peint et plastique en stuc dans la Lombardie du Xe–XIe siècle (résumé)." *Les Cahiers de Saint-Michel-de-Cuxa* 21, 1990, 109–13.

Perrin, Odet. *Les Burgondes: Leur histoire, des origines à la fin du premier royaume (534).* Neuchâtel, 1968.

Piquard, Maurice. *Jura, Franche-Comté, Belfort.* Paris, 1973.

Planat, P. *Encyclopédie de l'architecture et de la construction.* Paris, 7 vols., 1890.

Pognon, Edmond. *La Vie quotidienne en l'an mil.* Paris, 1981.

Poinssot, Claude. "Le Bâtiment du dortoir de l'abbaye de Saint-Bénigne de Dijon." *Bulletin monumental* 112, 1954, 303–30.

Poly, Jean-Pierre. *La Provence et la société féodale (879–1166).* Paris, 1976.

Ponsich, Pierre. "Complexité et originalité de l'art roman en Roussillon au XIe siècle: Saint-Martin de Tatzo-d'Avall en Roussillon Propre – l'avènement de l'architecture lombarde en Conflent." *Les Cahiers de Saint-Michel-de-Cuxa* 21, 1990, 7–27.

"L'Art de bâtir en Roussillon et en Cerdagne du IXe au XIIIe siècle." *Les Cahiers de Saint-Michel-de-Cuxa* 26, 1995, 35–56.

Porter, Arthur Kingsley. "Santa Maria Maggiore di Lomello." *Arte e Storia* 30, 1911, 175–81.

The Construction of Lombard and Gothic Vaults. New Haven, 1911.

Lombard Architecture. New Haven, 4 vols., 1917.

Poupardin, René. *Le Royaume de Bourgogne (888–1038): Étude sur les origines du royaume d'Arles.* Paris, 1907.

Le Royaume de Provence sous les Carolingiens (855–933). Marseille, 1974.

Prigent, Daniel, and Noël-Yves Tonnerre, eds. *La Construction en Anjou au Moyen Âge: Actes de la table ronde d'Angers des 29 et 30 mars 1996.* Angers, 1998.

Puig i Cadafalch, Josep. "Les Influences lombardes en Catalogne." *Congrès archéologique* 73, 1906, 684–703.

Santa Maria de la Seu d'Urgell. Barcelona, 1918.

"Decorative Forms of the First Romanesque Style." *Art Studies* 4, 1926, 11–99.

Le Premier Art roman. Paris, 1928.

La Géographie et les origines du premier art roman. Paris, 1935.

Quicherat, Jules. *Mélanges d'archéologie et d'histoire: Archéologie du Moyen Âge*. Paris, 1886, 74–85, 147–50.

Ragut, Camille. *Cartulaire de Saint-Vincent de Mâcon*. Mâcon, 1864.

Ranquet, E., and H. Ranquet. "Origine française du berceau roman." *Bulletin monumental* 90, 1931, 35–74.

Rave, Paul Ortwin. *Der Emporenbau in romanischer und frühgotischer Zeit*. Bonn, 1924.

Reveyron, Nicolas. "Culture technique et architecture monumentale: Analyse structurelle des types de contrefort dans l'architecture romane." In Patrice Beck, ed., *L'Innovation technique au Moyen Âge: Actes du VIe congrès international d'archéologie médiévale, 1–5 octobre 1996, Dijon*. Paris, 1998, 211–18.

"Les Nouvelles Approches de l'architecture médiévale." *Dossiers d'archéologie* 251, 2000, 2–5.

    ed. *Paray-le-Monial Brionnais-Charolais: Le Renouveau des études romanes; IIe colloque scientifique international de Paray-le-Monial (2–3–4 octobre 1998)*. Lonrai, 2000.

Rice, David Talbot. *The Great Palace of the Byzantine Emperors*. Edinburgh, 1958.

Richard, Jean. *Les Ducs de Bourgogne et la formation du duché du XIe au XIVe siècle*. Paris, 1954.

    ed. *Histoire de la Bourgogne*. Toulouse, 1978.

Riché, Pierre. *Écoles et enseignement dans le haut Moyen Âge, fin du Ve siècle–milieu du XIe siècle*. Paris, 1989.

Rivoira, Giovanni Teresio. *Lombardic Architecture: Its Origin, Development and Derivatives*. Trans. G. McN. Rushforth. London, 1910.

Roman Architecture. Trans. G. McN. Rushforth. London, 1925.

Roberti, Mario Mirabella. "Les Édifices préromans mineurs dans la vallée du Po." *Les Cahiers de Saint-Michel-de-Cuxa* 6, 1975, 167–80.

Rousset, Alphonse. *Dictionnaire géographique, historique et statistique des communes de Franche-Comté et des hameaux qui en dépendent, classés par département*. Besançon and Lons-le-Saunier, 1853–8.

Ruset, Danielle. *Monographie de l'église de Chapaize*. Mâcon, 1983.

Salet, Francis. "Cluny III." *Bulletin monumental* 126, 1968, 235–92.

Salmi, Mario. "Maestri comacini o commàcini?" *Artigianato e tecnica nella Società dell'alto medioevo occidentale: Settimane di Studi di Spoleto XVIII*. Spoleto, 1971, 1: 409–24; 2: 515–16.

Salvadori, Mario, and Robert Heller. *Structure in Architecture: The Building of Buildings*. Englewood Cliffs, N.J., 1963.

Salvadori, Mario, and Matthys Levy. *Structural Design in Architecture*. Englewood Cliffs, N.J., 1967.

Sanpaolesi, Piero. "Strutture a cupola autoportanti." *Palladio* 21, 1971, 3–64.

Sapin, Christian. *La Bourgogne préromane: Construction, décor et fonction des édifices religieux*. Paris, 1986.

"Bourgogne." In Xavier Barral i Altet, ed., *Le Paysage monumental de la France autour de l'an mil: Colloque international C.N.R.S., Hugues Capet 987–1987: La France de l'an mil, juin–septembre 1987*. Paris, 1987, 197–216.

"L'Ouverture *est* de la chapelle Saint-Michel de Tournus." *Société des Amis des Arts et des Sciences de Tournus* 86, 1987, 149–51.

"Saint-Bénigne de Dijon: Saint-Pierre de Flavigny et les ateliers de sculpture de la première moitié du XIe siècle." *Mémoires de la Commission des antiquités de la Côte-d'Or* 35, 1987–8, 215–42.

"Dendrochronologie et architecture monumentale dans le haut Moyen Âge; problèmes spécifiques." In Georges Lambert, ed., *Les Veines du temps: Lectures de bois en Bourgogne*. Autun, 1992, 159–75.

"L'Abbatiale de Gigny." In Annick Richard and Claudine Munier, eds., *Éclats d'histoire: 10 ans d'archéologie en Franche-Comté, 2500 ans d'héritages.* Besançon, 1995, 372–3.

"La Pierre et le voûtement: Innovation dans les techniques de construction des églises en Bourgogne au XIᵉ siècle." In Patrice Beck, ed., *L'Innovation technique au Moyen Âge: Actes du VIᵉ congrès international d'archéologie médiévale, 1–5 octobre 1996, Dijon.* Paris, 1998, 179–85.

"La Technique de construction en pierre autour de l'an mil, contribution à une réflexion et perspectives de recherches." In Daniel Prigent and Noël-Yves Tonnerre, eds., *La Construction en Anjou au Moyen Âge: Actes de la table ronde d'Angers des 29 et 30 mars 1996.* Angers, 1998, 13–31.

ed. *Les Prémices de l'art roman en Bourgogne: D'Auxerre à Cluny, les premiers édifices romans après l'an mil.* Auxerre, 1999.

Schapiro, Meyer. Review of Charles Oursel, *L'Art roman de Bourgogne,* in *Art Bulletin* 11, 1929, 227–8.

Schlink, Wilhelm. *Saint-Bénigne in Dijon: Untersuchungen zur Abteikirche Wilhelms von Volpiano (962–1031).* Berlin, 1978.

Segagni Malacart, Anna. "La 'Torre Civica' di Pavia e le torri campanarie padane del secolo XI." *Arte medievale* 4/2, 1990, 99–121.

Sennhauser, Hans Rudolf. *Romainmôtier und Payerne: Studien zur Cluniazenserarchitektur des 11. Jahrhunderts in der Westschweiz.* Basel, 1970.

Stalley, Roger. *Early Medieval Architecture.* Oxford, 1999.

Stimm, Helmut. *Studien zur Entwicklungsgeschichte des Frankoprovenzalischen.* Wiesbaden, 1952.

Straka, Georges, ed. *Les Dialectes de France au Moyen Âge et aujourd'hui: Domaines d'oïl et domaine franco-provençal.* Paris, 1972.

Sulser, Walter, with Alfred Heubach. "Die Restaurierung der Romanischen Kirche von Spiez." *Zeitschrift für schweizerische Archaeologie und Kunstgeschichte* 11/3, 1950, 1–18.

Sunderland, Alice L. "The Legend of the Alternate System at Saint-Bénigne of Dijon." *Journal of the Society of Architectural Historians* 18, 1958, 2–9.

Sunderland, Elizabeth R. *Charlieu à l'époque médiévale.* Lyons, 1971.

Testi, Laura Cristiani. "L'arco acuto in Francia nei secoli XI e XII, e le coincidenze con le architetture monastiche in Italia." *Critica d'arte* 11, 1964, 19–30.

Thirion, Jacques, "L'Église Saint-Dalmas de Valdeblore." *Bulletin monumental* 111, 1953, 157–71.

"Un Témoin du premier art roman en Provence: La Madone de Levens." *Bulletin monumental* 119, 1961, 345–51.

"Au début de l'architecture romane en Provence: L'ancienne église de Saint-Donat." *Bulletin monumental* 73, 1965, 271–94.

"L'Influence lombarde dans les Alpes françaises du sud." *Bulletin monumental* 128, 1970, 7–40.

"L'Influence de l'Italie du Nord sur l'art roman de la Provence orientale." *Atti del II Congresso storico Liguria-Provenza, Grasse, ottobre 1968.* Bordighera-Aix-Marseille, 1971, 37–60.

"Remarques sur la crypte et les structures récemment dégagées de l'église de Saint-Dalmas-Valdeblore." *Cahiers archéologiques* 38, 1990, 63–79.

ed. *Saint-Philibert de Tournus: Histoire, archéologie, art. Actes du colloque du Centre International d'Études Romanes, Tournus, 15–19 juin 1994.* Mâcon, 1995.

Thümmler, Hans. "Die Baukunst des 11. Jahrhunderts in Italien." *Römisches Jahrbuch für Kunstgeschichte* 3, 1939, 141–226.

Thurlby, Malcolm. "Observations on Romanesque and Gothic Vault Construction." *Arris* 6, 1995, 22–9.

Tibaldi, Tancredi Giuseppe. *La Vallée d'Aoste au Moyen Âge.* Turin, 1886.

Toubert, Pierre. *Études sur l'Italie médiévale (IXᵉ–XIVᵉ s.).* London, 1976.

Tournier, René. "Aspects de l'architecture religieuse en Franche-Comté." *Congrès archéologique* 118, 1960, 9–17.

   "Gigny." *Congrès archéologique* 118, 1960, 168–75.

   Franche-Comté romane. Pierre-qui-vire, 1979.

Traversi, Gino. *Architettura paleocristiana milanese.* Milan, 1964.

Truchis, Pierre de. "Les Influences orientales dans l'architecture romane de la Bourgogne." *Congrès archéologique* 74, 1907, 459–500.

   "L'Architecture lombarde: Ses origines, son extension dans le centre, l'est et le midi de la France." *Congrès archéologique* 76, 1909, 204–42.

Vallery-Radot, Jean. "Le Premier Art roman de l'Occident méditerranéen (à propos d'un livre récent)." *La Revue de l'art ancien et moderne* 55, 1929, 105–22, 153–69.

   "Le Domaine de l'école romane de Provence." *Bulletin monumental* 113, 1945, 5–63.

   "Introduction à l'histoire des églises de la Suisse romande des origines au milieu du XIIIᵉ siècle." *Congrès archéologique* 110, 1952, 12–16.

   Saint-Philibert de Tournus. Paris, 1955.

   "L'Église de Saint-Hymetière." *Congrès archéologique* 118, 1960, 153–65.

   "Saint-Jean-de-Maurienne, la cathédrale Saint-Jean-Baptiste." *Congrès archéologique* 123, 1965, 49–85.

   "La Cathédrale Saint-Pierre à Moûtiers-en-Tarentaise." *Congrès archéologique* 123, 1965, 106–20.

   "L'Église Saint-Martin à Aime." *Congrès archéologique* 123, 1965, 121–36.

Varaldo, Carlo. *La chiesa di San Paragorio a Noli e la zona archeologica.* Savona, 1978.

Vergnolle, Eliane. *L'Art roman en France.* Paris, 1994.

   "Les Débuts de l'art roman dans le royaume franc (ca. 980–ca. 1020)." *Cahiers de civilisation médiévale* 43/2, 2000, 161–94.

Verzone, Paolo. *L'architettura romanica nel vercellese.* Vercelli, 1934

   L'architettura romanica nel novarese. Novara, 2 vols., 1935–6.

   "L'origine della volta lombarda a nervature." *Atti del IV Convegno nazionale di storia dell'architettura, Milano, 18–25 giugno 1939.* Milan, 1941, 53–64.

   L'architettura religiosa dell'alto medioevo nell'Italia settentrionale. Milan, 1942.

Veyret, Germaine, and Paul Veyret. "Essai de définition de la montagne." *Revue de géographie alpine* 50, 1962, 5–37.

Vicini, Donata. "Correlazioni tra il romanico ligure e il romanico provenzale." In Piero Sanpaolesi, ed., *Il Romanico: Atti del Seminario di studi diretto da Piero Sanpaolesi, Villa Monastero di Varenna, 8–16 settembre 1973.* Milan, 1975, 225–37.

Vigué, Jordi, et al. "Sant Vicenç de Cardona." *Catalunya romànica,* vol. 11: *El Bages.* Barcelona, 1989, 151–71

Viollet-le-Duc, Eugène Emmanuel. *Dictionnaire raisonné de l'architecture française du XIᵉ au XVIᵉ siècle.* Paris, 10 vols., 1854–68.

Virey, Jean. "L'Église de Chapaize." *Annales de l'Académie de Mâcon* 27, 1930–1, 437–44.

   Les Églises romanes de l'ancien diocèse de Mâcon: Cluny et sa région. Mâcon, 1935.

   Saint-Philibert de Tournus. Paris, 1954.

Vregille, Bernard. "Les Origines chrétiennes et le Haut Moyen Âge." In Claude Fohlen, ed., *Histoire de Besançon*. Paris, 1964, 231–4.

Vuarnet, Émile. *Patois de Savoie, Dauphiné et Suisse*. Thonon, 1907.

Ward-Perkins, John B. *Roman Imperial Architecture*. Harmondsworth, 1981.

Wartburg, Walther von. *Les Origines des peuples romans*. (Trans. of *Die Entstehung der romanischen Völker*.) Paris, 1941.

Willis, Robert. "On the Construction of the Vaults of the Middle Ages." *Transactions of the Royal Institute of British Architects, London*, 1, 1842, 1–69.

Zanotto, Andrea. *Aoste: Histoire, antiquités, objects d'art*. Aosta, 1967.

Histoire de la Vallée d'Aoste. Aosta, 1968.

Zastrow, Oleg. *L'arte romanica del comasco*. Como, 1972.

"Architettura romanica nel Lecchese, nel Comasco, in Valtellina e in Valchiavenna: Connessioni e contrasti." *Archivi di Lecco* 12/3, 1989, 395–444.

Zimarino, Nicola. *Les Cintres pour voûtes: Méthodes générales de calcul et types de construction*. Paris, 1963.

Index

Note: Illustration pages are shown in boldface italics.